CHRISTIAN ASHRAMS

A NEW RELIGIOUS MOVEMENT

IN CONTEMPORARY INDIA

Helen Ralston

Studies in Religion and Society
Volume 20

The Edwin Mellen Press
Lewiston/Queenston

Library of Congress Cataloging-in-Publication Data

Ralston, Helen.
  Christian ashrams : a new religious movement in contemporary India
/ Helen Ralston.
    p. cm.-- (Studies in religion and society : v. 20)
  Bibliography: p.
  Includes index.
  ISBN 0-88946-854-0
  1. Christian communities--India--History--20th century.
2. Ashrams--India--History--20th century. 3. Monasteries--India-
-History--20th century. 4. India--Church history. I. Title.
II. Series: Studies in religion and society (New York, N.Y.) : v.
20.
  BV4406.I4R35 1987
  250'.954--dc19   87-21019
                                                              CIP

This is volume 20 in the continuing series
Studies in Religion and Society
Volume 20 ISBN 0-88946-854-0
SRS Series ISBN 0-88946-863-X

The Edwin Mellen Press   The Edwin Mellen Press
Box 450   Box 67
Lewiston, New York   Queenston, Ontario
USA 14092   CANADA LOS 1LO

Printed in the United States of America

For Sophia

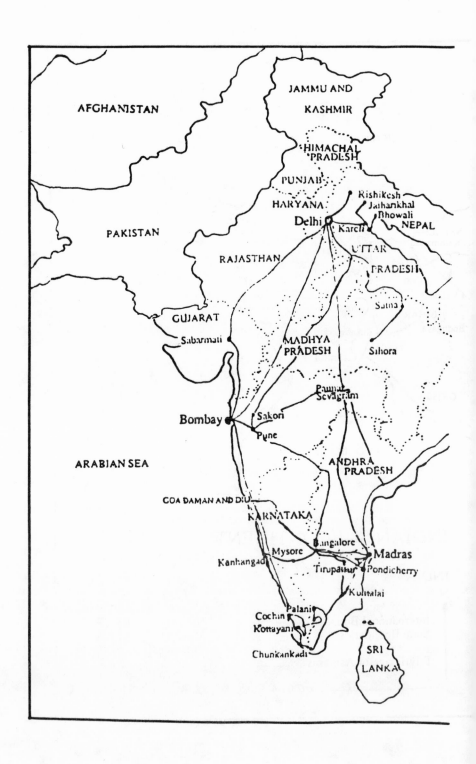

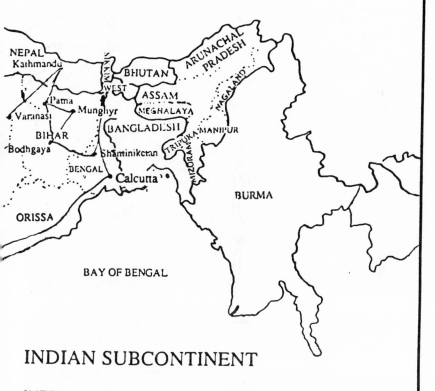

CHINA

NEPAL
Kathmandu

SIKKIM
BHUTAN
ARUNACHAL PRADESH

WEST
ASSAM
NAGALAND

Patna
Munghyr
MEGHALAYA

Varanasi
BANGLADESH
MANIPUR

BIHAR
TRIPURA
MIZORAM

Bodhgaya
Shantiniketan

BENGAL
Calcutta

BURMA

ORISSA

BAY OF BENGAL

INDIAN SUBCONTINENT

INDIA

N

International Boundaries ▬▬
State Boundaries ┄┄

Pilgrimage of Ashrams ▬▬

├────┴────┴────┤ 600 km.

Area 3,287,782 sq. km.
Population (1984) 712 million
Hindus   ·83.0%
Muslims   11.0%
Christians   2.6%
Sikhs   2.0%
Buddhists   0.7%
Jains   0.4%
Other   0.3%

CONTENTS

PREFACE

A 'passage to India' in a sabbatical year! Who could resist it? The invitation to give some lectures in India in the latter part of 1979 led me to study Christianity as a minority religion in India. As a sociologist, I readily accepted the assumption that the social and cultural forms of Christianity in Asia, Africa and Latin America had been imported as baggage of the various colonizers. A preliminary pilot study in 1979 of ashrams as an inculturation movement among Christians raised the more precise research questions which I address in this book. How does one account for the emergence, rise, persistence or decline of Christian ashrams in India? What are the social processes involved in the so-called 'ashram movement'? Why is it called a movement?

It was Vandana Mātāji, RSCJ, a leader of the Catholic ashram movement and founder of Jeevan Dhara ashram, together with Ishpriya Mātāji, RSCJ, also of Jeevan Dhara ashram, and Sara Grant, RSCJ, Achārya of Christa Prema Seva ashram, who first introduced me to ashrams as a mode of inculturation of Christian spirituality and life-style. As members of my own international religious congregation, they led me to question a definition of internationality which is limited to Western society and excludes the rest of the world. I owe them a deep debt of gratitude. Not only did they invite me to their ashrams, to conferences, workshops and retreats, but they also introduced me to countless ashram leaders, Catholic, Protestant and Hindu. I am sure that they will disagree with some of my interpretations and conclusions; nevertheless, the research would have impossible without their assistance.

In the course of the discussion of various ashrams throughout the book, I acknowledge interviews with many individuals. I thank these persons and the other unnamed ashram members who so willingly gave me their time and attention, as well as hospitality. I would also like to thank the faculty and staff of the Vidyajyoti Institute of Religious Studies, Delhi, for allowing me to use their library virtually twenty-four hours a day and seven days a week, and for sheltering and feeding me in the horrendous riots following the assassination of Indira Gandhi on October 31, 1984. In particular, I thank Fr. George Gispert-Sauch, S.J., for his invaluable bibliographical assistance and his untiring good humour.

Dr. Peter Beyer of The Edwin Mellen Press, Dr. Dick Taylor (a long-time student of Christian ashrams) of the Christian Institute for the Study of Religion and Society, New Delhi and Bangalore, and Dr. Ursula King of the University of Leeds all made very helpful comments on the first draft of the manuscript. I thank them for their contributions. The final manuscript is my own responsibility.

I am grateful also to Margaret Boyd for proof-reading the penultimate draft of the manuscript and to Cheryl Blynn for invaluable technical assistance with the microcomputer.

The research was made possible by a Fellowship of the Shastri Indo-Canadian Institute, held between October 2, 1983, and June 2, 1984, and between October 2, 1984, and March 2, 1985. A Saint Mary's University Senate Research Grant supplemented those funds. I am grateful to Saint Mary's University for granting me an additional leave (over and above a regular sabbatical year) to complete field work and library research in India.

Helen Ralston

May 12, 1987

CHAPTER 1

INTRODUCTION

Since the 1960s there has been considerable sociological interest in the emergence in North America and in Europe of new religious movements which have been imported from India and the Orient.[1] Few scholars have examined Christianity as an intrusive and alien religion in India; even fewer have studied the impact of Hinduism and of Indian social movements on Christianity.[2] Such is the focus of this book. It looks at the emergence and development of Christian ashrams as a new religious movement which seeks to amalgamate elements of traditional Christianity and traditional Hinduism in contemporary Indian society.[3]

2 Christian Ashrams

The major research for the study was conducted in India over a period of fourteen months, from October 1983 to May 1984 inclusive, and from October 1984 to March 1985 inclusive. The research was based on a variety of field methods, including participant observation in Hindu and Christian ashrams, as well as interviews with Hindu and Christian religious leaders and with persons knowledgeable about ashrams. In all, I visited twenty Hindu ashrams and thirty-one Christian ashrams. A list of the ashrams visited is contained in Appendices I and II. The map of India traces my pilgrimage of ashrams.

It is difficult to assess the exact number of Christian ashrams existent today. I did not conduct a survey of all Christian ashrams. Michael O'Toole (1983) has produced a directory and guide of thirty-nine Christian ashrams. On the one hand, however, he has included some communities which are questionably identified as ashrams; while on the other hand, he has omitted many ashrams; for example, the Orthodox Syrian ashrams in Kerala and the Lutheran ashrams of Subbama (1970, 1973) in Andhra Pradesh. Although it is common among ashramites and others to speak of two classes of Christian ashrams, namely, Protestant and Catholic, my field work has indicated that other Christian groups, such as Orthodox Syrian, Mar Thoma, Lutheran and Ecumenical groups, have established ashram communities.

Although the Christian ashram movement began in the early part of this century, prior to Indian independence, it was not until the post-independence era that ashram associations were formed. There are two associations of Christian ashrams: (1) the Inter Ashram Fellowship;[4] and (2) the Ashram Aikiya.[5] The former was founded in the late forties, with the first regular annual meeting of the Fellowship being held in 1949. Admission to membership is based on "the characteristics of the common life of an ashram."[6] In 1974 a Medical Wing of nine members of the Inter Ashram Fellowship was formed to co-ordinate the medical and health work of the ashrams and fellowships. The membership of the Fellowship is inter-denominational and includes ashrams in Sri Lanka and Nepal as well as India. In all there are twenty-two members of the Inter Ashram Fellowship, comprising the following ashrams: one Orthodox Syrian, eleven Protestant, five Mar Thoma, three Catholic and two Ecumenical.

The Ashram Aikiya was founded much later (in 1978) and is composed exclusively of Catholic ashrams. There are about thirty *ashram* members of the

Aikiya.[7] Membership of the Ashram Aikiya, however, is on an individual basis, including those who presently live in an ashram, those who have had the experience of living in an ashram, and those who are sympathetic to the ashram ideal. In contrast, membership of the Inter Ashram Fellowship is made up of *representatives,* not exceeding two, from each ashram which is recognized as a member of the association.[8]

All the Christian ashrams are small communities. The number of permanent members in an ashram varies from only one person in several Catholic ashrams, to a maximum of sixteen members (at Christa Panthi ashram, Sihora, Madhya Pradesh), with the average membership being eight or less.[9] The Orthodox Syrian ashrams and convents have a somewhat larger membership, but not all members reside in the main dwelling.

What is an *ashram* ? The question is posed not only by those who are unfamiliar with Indian cultural traditions, but even by ashramites themselves. An *ashram* is typically described as a spontaneous community of seekers or disciples gathered around a spiritual leader, called a *guru,* who points a way to salvation. This conception of ashram draws heavily on the *asrāma* theory of sanskrit writers in its reference to a way of life characterized by meditation, asceticism and strenuous endeavour in all stages of life (Kane, 1941:425). As a researcher, one sometimes senses a certain resistance among ashramites toward generalizations about ashrams, and even toward identification of what is, or is not, a "real ashram." Each ashram tends to be regarded as a unique spontaneous community (Jones, 1939:200; Chandy, 1983:4; Griffiths, 1984:150). Life in an ashram is characterized by simplicity, discipline and community of goods. It will normally include elements of the three traditional Indian spiritual paths of meditation, devotion, and selfless service or action. The Constitution of the Inter Ashram Fellowship notes that ancient Indian ashrams were centres of study, research, contemplation and experimentation, where there was a marked breaking-down of barriers of culture, caste, class, race and creeds. The Ashram Aikiya emphasizes that an ashram is a place of an intense and sustained spiritual quest.[10]

In the ideology of the Christian ashram movement, the charismatic guru is identified as the central religious personality from whose personal religious experience and inspiration the ashram is created, and upon whose authority the guru-disciple relationship is based (Vandana, 1978b:51-2; Griffiths, 1982:24). The conceptualization of ashram, guru and guru-disciple relationship in both Hindu and Christian writings appears to lay great emphasis on charismatic authority, in which the power to command is legitimated by the extraordinary qualities of grace believed to rest in a person. The model, as presented in much of the literature, tends to describe the individual guru as *the* essential constituent element of the ashram, to the neglect of the guru-disciple *relationship* as the key structural element and *necessary* condition for the creation of the community. In contrast to this approach, I argue, with Weber (and others), that charismatic authority is socially constructed in the recognition, acceptance and legitimation by followers of the extraordinary qualities of a leader who articulates a message expressing their consciousness, values and interests. Any attempt to understand the emergence and development of the Christian ashram movement must therefore take into account the historical and socio-cultural context from which it emerged, the structure of social relationships in the movement, as well as the contributions of leadership and ideology to the emergence, persistence or decline of the movement.

In Chapter 2, I elaborate this theoretical argument. For methodological and theoretical enlightenment I draw on the body of literature which considers new religious movements as particular kinds of social movements. In Chapter 3, I consider the historico-social context out of which the Christian ashram movement emerged: the intrusion of Christianity into India; the evident socio-political contradictions of Indian society; the concerns for socio-political transformation; the emergence of the Neo-Hindu reform movements and of the nationalist movement; the challenges to existing assumptions about the nature of Hinduism and of Christianity, and of the relationship between them; the new conceptions of modes of church structure and organization.

In Chapter 4, I examine the contribution of leadership and ideologies to the emergence of the Protestant and Catholic ashram movements, respectively. In Chapter 5, I identify key Hindu concepts which have been appropriated and adapted to traditional Christianity by the Christian ashram movement. In Chapter 6, I describe some contemporary Hindu ashrams which exemplify the different *mārgas* or ways which can be followed towards salvation. In Chapters 7 and 8, I examine Christian ashrams in terms of their expression of the three principal Hindu ways of action, devotion, and knowledge, respectively. Finally, I assess the significance of the Christian ashram movement in contemporary Indian society.

The study of the Christian ashram movement as a movement for the indigenization of Christianity within the Indian socio-religious context offers interesting insights into the specific problem of how interaction with the Hindu religious consciousness has modified the Christian consciousness to produce a new kind of religious community in India. It also sheds light on the historical and socio-cultural conditions which have led to the emergence of these groups. The study also contributes to an understanding of the more general problem of the relationship between religious movements and social change.

Notes

[1]Some of the outstanding works include the following: Wilson's (1979) study of indigenously controlled movements, of movements inspired by external contacts, and of sects in Third World countries directed from Western countries; Glock and Bellah's (1976) collection of essays; Cox's (1977) study of Asian religious influence in the United States. Robbins, Anthony and Richardson (1978) present an extensive bibliography of theory and research on new religions; Needleham and Baker (1978) deal with new religious movements in the United States; Robertson (1979) discusses the relationship between modern religious movements and American society; Barker (1982) presents a collection of essays on new religious movements in Europe and the United States. Barker (1986) gives an overview of theoretical and empirical work in the study of new religious movements since 1978. Beckford (1986) discusses the development of new religious movements in eight countries undergoing rapid social change; he includes an essay by Sharma (1986), which deals with new religious movements in India. Ralston (1988) presents an overview of the study of new religious movements in Canada by anglophone and francophone sociologists.

[2]Immanuel (1950) has studied the influence of Hinduism on South Indian Christians. He argues that Indian Christians have inherited customs, beliefs and thought forms from their Hindu background. He describes some Hindu and Christian ashrams and discusses the place of Christian ashrams as experimental and prophetic groups in the church.

[3]To my knowledge, Taylor (1977) is the only sociologist to have suggested a typology for describing and understanding Christian ashrams. Taylor's use of *khadi* (home-spun cloth) and *kavi* (ochre-coloured cloth), as symbols for two polarized ideal-types of ashram, is helpful. As Taylor (1977:19-20) points out, *khadi* is a potent symbol of the Gandhian nationalist movement. It signifies spinning, self-reliance *(swâraj)* and solidarity with the country by the use of home-

produced goods*(swadeshi);* in other words, an engagement with the world in selfless action. *Kavi* , on the other hand, symbolizes renunciation of the world and dedication to a life of meditation or contemplation. It signifies identification with the ancient Hindu religious tradition, as exemplified in the Neo-Hindu reform movements.

[4]Information about the Inter Ashram Fellowship comes from the following sources: (a) the Constitution, passed at the annual business meeting held on 12 December, 1982, and published in *Inter Ashram Review*, February, 1983; (b) subsequent issues of *Inter Ashram Review*, which is privately circulated among the membership; (c) conversations with members of the Fellowship. I attended the annual meeting of the Inter Ashram Fellowship at the Christian Fellowship Community Health Centre, Ambilikkai, Tamil Nadu, 10-11 February, 1984.

[5]The Ashram Aikiya began as a result of the "get-together and live-together" of twenty ashramites, which was held at the National Biblical, Catechetical and Liturgical Centre (NBCLC), Bangalore, 5-7 June, 1978, and which was followed by an All-India Consultation on Ashrams, with about one hundred participants (Vandana, 1978c:358; Amalorpavadass, 1984:306). Both meetings were convened by the Liturgical Commission of the Catholic Bishops Conference of India. The first meeting of June, 1978, is referred to as Ashram Aikiya Satsang I. Ashram Aikiya Satsang II was held at *Shāntivanam* ashram, Kulittalai, Tamil Nadu, 4-7 December, 1980; Satsang III was held at NBCLC, Bangalore, 18-22 October, 1983; Satsang IV was held at *Anjali* ashram, Mysore, 25-29 November, 1985. I was one of seventy-five participants who attended Satsang III; among them were nine Hindu and Protestant guests, who addressed the gathering. The Ashram Aikiya produces an informal newsletter twice a year for its membership.

[6]From the Constitution of the Inter Ashram Fellowship.

[7]Information provided by Father Matthew Lederle, S.J., secretary of the Ashram Aikiya at the time of my research, and by Sri Anil Sequiera, who was responsible for publication of the *Ashram Aikiya Newsletter*. An ashram may comprise a community of several members or only one person (a *guru*) who has a few followers living with him or her from time to time.

[8]From the Constitution, published in *Inter Ashram Review*, February 1983, p. 25.

[9]I did not conduct a survey of all Christian ashrams. Twelve ashrams were represented at the annual Inter Ashram Fellowship meeting, which I attended, at Ambilikkai, 10-11 February, 1984; twenty-six ashrams were represented at Ashram Aikiya Satsang III, which I attended, at Bangalore, 18-22 October, 1983. I collected data on membership at both of these meetings. I also checked my estimate of average ashram membership with Reverend P. T, Thomas, Achärya of Christävashram, Mangänam, and President of the Inter Ashram Fellowship, in a personal interview on 23 January, 1985. P. T. Thomas has recently conducted a survey of non-Catholic ashrams, which will be published in Malayalam.

[10]*Statement of the All-India Consultation on Ashrams, 7th to 11th June, 1978.* Statement Series No.22 of the National Biblical, Catechetical and Liturgical Centre, Bangalore.

CHAPTER 2

THEORETICAL CONSIDERATIONS

Religion may be defined as a form of consciousness which refers to a reality which is non-empirical to make sense of an empirical world. In so doing, the religious consciousness expresses symbolically the lived relationship of people with their world.[1] To understand religion in any society, one must first understand the complexities of the social, economic, historical and existential elements of the human situation in that society, and how people express their interpretations of those complexities in religious consciousness. The actual mode of consciousness depends upon the kind of explanation religion offers for the existing reality and the kind of responses it projects for resolving any experienced contradictions.[2] In the face of evident contradictions in the world, the religious consciousness can be expressed in different symbols, rituals, rhetoric, interpretations, and organization, in different orientations to the world and to social change, and in different types of religious movements. In other words, religion, and religious movements, are socially situated and socially constructed in the context of the historical and social relationships of a society.

At the same time, religion is only partially produced by the social structure. It is also relatively autonomous in structuring the collective experience and the collective consciousness of a group. It has its own sets of social relationships and develops its own conflictive dynamics. Moreover, religion, insofar as it shapes the consciousness, identity and relationships of its believers, is an active element in structuring society.[3]

The large body of research on religious movements, particularly new religious movements, has offered various explanations to account for their emergence.[4] For the most part, religious movements are assumed to be attempts to deal with the inadequacies of existing religious institutional structures in the context of broad systemic change and strain in the institutional structure and value-system of society. Various types of relative deprivation are described to explain why frustrated or deviant individuals are attracted to religious movements.[5] There is little support, however, for the relative deprivation thesis in Western society, particularly when it is interpreted in terms of economic deprivation, since those who join new religious movements in Europe and in North America tend to be educated, middle-class individuals.[6] An alternative approach has been to link the emergence of different types of religious movements with secularization of society (Stark and Bainbridge, 1979). Quite apart from criticisms of the secularization thesis on theoretical grounds (notably by Wallis and Bruce, 1984), this approach is more applicable to North American and European society than to India.

Some studies have drawn on various paradigms offered by the social movements literature to explain the emergence and success or decline of religious movements.[7] The classic approach to the study of social movements has laid great emphasis on broad shifts in societal values, and on charismatic leaders and ideologies as the key factors in the emergence of the movements.[8] There has been a tendency to pay little attention to the history of a particular society and to the tensions and contradictions in the larger societal structure, and, indeed, in the global society, which are intimately related to such value shifts and ideological constructions, and which make the movements attractive to their followers. Such has been the case in the study of Neo-Hindu reform movements of the nineteenth and early twentieth centuries, of post-independence new Hindu religious movements, of the Hindu and Christian ashram movements, and, to some extent, of the Indian nationalist movement.

In recent years, alternative explanations have been offered. The resource-mobilization paradigm directs attention to the variety (e.g., people, money, facilities, labour and associations) and sources of resources which can be mobilized in support of movements and movement organizations.[9] Another paradigm attempts to explain social movements in a world-system framework. When applied to religious movements, this perspective analyzes religious movements in terms of critical changes in the world economic order: the type of movement that emerges varies according to whether the adherents are centrally or peripherally related to the sources of world economic power.[10]

There has been considerable criticism of theoretical approaches which emphasize charismatic leaders and ideologies as the key explanatory elements in movement formation. Several sociologists[11] have pointed out that Weber's concept of charisma denotes not so much a quality of the individual as of *a relationship* between the leader and the followers or disciples. Weber (1968:244,1112-3) makes it quite clear that charismatic authority is socially constructed. The extraordinary qualities of the leader, recognized, accepted and legitimated by the followers, are transformed into authority. Worsley (1968:xiv) regards the qualities of leaders and the loyalty of followers "as marginal items in the explanation of social movements and their consequences." He is more impressed by the quality of the message articulated by the leaders and its appropriateness to the awakened consciousness of exploited classes. Liebman (1983:237) takes a similar position when he argues that "(m)ovement leaders give voice to widely held discontents and *give shape to* calls for change" (my emphasis).

Worsley (1968:ix-xxi) has modified and elaborated Weber's (1968:244,1112-3) seminal analysis of charismatic authority to conceptualize and explain the processes of movement formation. Worsley (1968:xviii) speaks of the charismatic leader as "a catalytic personality who strikes responsive chords in his audience." For Worsley (1968:xv,xxxv), the charismatic leader and the followers are partners in a relationship which is oriented to action. The social significance of the leader is as "symbol, catalyst and message-bearer" (Worsley, 1968:xvii). The leader's catalytic function is "to convert latent solidarities into active ritual and political action" (Worsley, 1968:xviii). An audience which responds to the leader's message becomes a following, then a movement, and finally an organization (Worsley, 1968:xxxvi). Maduro (1982:107) sees the charismatic leader as "rendering explicit what is implicit, ... uniting what is disunited, ... formulating, in words and deeds, a set of unsatisfied religious demands." The followers find their unsatisfied demands expressed in the leader's formulation. They can "mobilize their energies around the (charismatic leader's) words and deeds." New religious movements tend to emerge when religious leaders articulate a message which is recognized as expressing the consciousness, values and interests of the audience. In a similar line of argument, Liebman (1983:237) notes that movement leaders frequently "marshall resources and devise strategies."

According to Liebman (1983:237-8), explanations of the emergence of social movements must take cognizance of the socio-cultural environment as the seed-bed of the movement. He emphasizes that in no sense do social movements originate as full-blown ideologies in the minds of leaders. Religious movements may play a part in the struggle of subordinate groups against internal or external domination. However, they germinate and flourish only when they provide their adherents with explanations for the problems of everyday life and with possibilities for their resolution. Their emergence depends less on the subjective consciousness and intentions of their agents than on the objective conditions in which the agents are operating. The message articulated by the leaders must be recognized by the listeners and followers as relevant to the perceived contradictions in the socio-cultural environment.

A particular religious movement can be understood and analyzed only in a concrete and determinate historical and social context. Hence the sociologist must focus attention on history and on the socio-cultural environment, which provide the context of changed meanings in value-systems, rather than on changed ideologies in isolation from the socio-cultural and historical context. Liebman also claims that a social movement, rather than being an instrument of social change, is an indicator of once current concerns. Be that as it may, it is certainly true, as Maduro (1982:119) insists, that the particular functions of a particular social (or religious) movement in a particular socio-historical context can only be established *a posteriori*.

I have applied this conceptual framework to my analysis of the Christian ashram movement. I assume that the history and the structure of social relationships of Christian communities in India is part of the national history and the social construction of relationships of the Indian people as a whole.[12] I reject social deprivation explanations for the emergence of the Christian ashram movement. Rather, I perceive religion as a dynamic agent in structuring and producing a meaning-system and a sociability structure which are more plausible and more in tune with a new mode of consciousness, a new world-view. For some Christian Indians, at least, the existing insitutionalized forms of Indian Christianity were experienced as alienated from the rich Indian religious and cultural heritage and as a particular expression of cultural imperialism in a colonial situation. The world-system approach offers some helpful insights in this regard, for it locates Indian people in a peripheral position in a global political and economic order.

The Christian ashram movement was the product of a new religious consciousness in a specific Indian historico-social context. It highlighted (indicated, in Liebman's terms) the religious and political tensions within Indian society, and within the Christian Indian community in particular, in the early twentieth century. It reflected a new world-view among a colonized people seeking liberation from the colonial structures of society. At the same time, the Christian ashram movement, as a particular expression of the general Indian Christianity movement, found its identity in its relationship with the nationalist movement and thus played a part in the Indian struggle for independence from colonial domination. Leaders correctly perceived and understood the meaning of these social, cultural and political tensions. They regarded religion and politics as interrelated. They articulated a message which fell on the receptive ears of an audience with a consciousness awakened to the contradictions in the existing political and socio-cultural situation. In other words, they "gave shape to" the call for change and presented a model of a new form of Christian organization which attempted to integrate traditional Christianity and traditional Hinduism and to construct new patterns of social relationships. The Christian ashram movement was socially created and constructed in the relationship between leaders and followers. As it developed, the movement recruited members, mobilized resources and devised strategies to create a new religious order which was perceived as more appropriate for Christian Indians in a society which was actively moving toward national independence.

In post-independence India, not only is the religious situation changed, but the political and socio-cultural situation is different. The growth and development of the Christian ashram movement can be understood only in the context of these changed religious, political and socio-cultural conditions. In the final chapter, I will discuss the implications of national independence and contemporary world views for the Christian ashram movement.

Notes

[1]The classical theorists have expressed this general understanding of religion in a variety of ways. For Durkheim (1964:422-23, 427), religion is in fact a mirror which reflects society's consciousness of itself, its collective ideal and cultural dream which have their sources in life; for Marx (Marx and Engels, 1964:41-2), it is a false consciousness which masks the contradictions in society; for Freud (1964:47-53), religion is an illusion which reflects neurotic childhood frustrations; for Weber (1958b:218), it is a mode of creating a 'meaningful cosmos' out of a world which is 'experienced as specifically senseless.' Among contemporary theorists, Geertz (1976:3) finds that religion as a cultural system synthesizes a people's world view and in so doing makes their life seem intelligible and meaningful; Berger (1969:25) defines religion as 'the human enterprise by which a sacred cosmos is established;' for Alves (1984), religion is a profound emotional experience of the meaning of life.

[2]Weber's (1958c) Protestant ethic thesis and comparative studies of religion bring out the effects of different forms of religious orientation and motivation on ways of seeking salvation (Weber, 1968:576-634) and on modes of religious organization (Weber, 1968:56,1164); Durkheim (1964:423) has recognized that society's conflicts over its conception of itself arise 'not between the ideal and reality but between different ideals, that of yesterday and that of today, that which has authority of tradition and that which has the hope of the future.' For Marx (Marx and Engels, 1964:42), religion is indeed 'the opium of the people,' but even for him, the false consciousness of religion is not merely 'an expression of real distress but at the same time the protest against distress.' In other words, the religious consciousness includes critical questioning of reality. Rubem Alves (1971) has

provided important insights on the relation between religious consciousness and social reality, particularly in the Latin American context.

[3]Otto Maduro (1982) develops this thesis with respect to Latin American society.

[4]Beckford (1977) reviewed approaches to explaining the emergence of religious movements in research up to the mid-seventies. Barker (1986) has brought the review up to the mid-eighties.

[5]One of the clearest statements on the different types of religious movements which emerge to compensate persons for various kinds of deprivation is that of Glock and Stark (1965).

[6]Wallis (1975) presents a succinct critique of the relative deprivation thesis.

[7]Ramirez (1981) examines three paradigms (namely, the social-integration, the resource-mobilization, and the world-system paradigms) which have been used for the study of social movements and shows how they have been applied to the study of religious movements.

[8]See, for example, Heberle (1968:438-44).

[9]McCarthy and Zald (1977) and Jenkins (1983) present expositions of the resource-mobilization paradigm. Bromley and Shupe (1980), Richardson (1982), Bromley (1985) and Bird and Westley (1985) have used this approach to study the mobilization of financial resources for new religious movements. Hadden and Swann (1981) and Liebman and Wuthnow (1983) have discussed at some length the mobilization of conservative Christians, financial resources and political action committees in support of the New Christian Right. Wolcott (1982) has also used the resource mobilization approach to analyze the mobilization of an ecumenical coalition against a steel conglomerate.

[10]The world-system paradigm is postulated by Wallerstein (1976). Wuthnow (1978, 1980) and Anthony and Robbins (1978) have applied the paradigm to the study of religious movements.

[11]See, for example, the following: Blau (1963:307); Worsley (1968:xxxv); Wilson, (1975:7); Theobald (1980:84); Wallis(1982:38).

[12]Thomas (1979:11) takes this position. He argues that "the assumption that Christians have a separate history... is both a distortion of history as such, and a distortion of the historical facts related to them."

CHAPTER 3

THE ASHRAM MOVEMENT:

HISTORICO-SOCIAL BACKGROUND

Christianity[1] was introduced as an alien religion into the religiously plural society of India. It was brought in three main movements, the first two being historically separated by some fourteen hundred years. The first movement, soon after the death of Christ (led by St. Thomas the Apostle, according to tradition), was the East Syrian Christian movement of traders and merchants, who made converts and established settlements of Christians on the south-west Kerala coast of India. The second movement came from western Europe in the late fifteenth and sixteenth centuries, when the Portuguese, in their voyages of discovery, took control of the trade centres and established colonies. The Portuguese brought priests who introduced a Roman Catholic form of Christianity which had accommodated itself to Greco-Roman culture but which made no attempt to accommodate itself to Indian culture.[2] The third major Christian movement was the British and American Protestant missionary expansion during Britain's colonial period. The first true Protestant mission in Asia was the Danish Lutheran mission, which was started in 1706 at Tranquebar along the Coromandel coast in south-east India, where Denmark had established trading settlements (Varghese and Philip, 1983:53-5). Some Protestant chaplains had also arrived with the British East India Company in the latter part of the seventeenth century, but it was under direct rule by the British government in the late nineteenth and early twentieth centuries that Protestant missionaries arrived in great numbers and that Christianity saw its greatest growth as a powerful religious movement in India.[3] Various missionary societies became active in establishing schools, colleges and medical services, besides churches; for example, the London Missionary Society (L.M.S.) of the Congregational churches in south India, and the Church Missionary Society (C.M.S.) and the Society for Propagating the Gospel (S.P.G.) of the Anglican Church, which worked throughout India. Christianity remained, however, very much a minority religion, with Christians representing only 1.24% of the population in 1911 (Weber, 1958a:5), and then rising to somewhat more than 2% in the period of greatest growth (Schermerhorn, 1978:183-7).

The term *Christian* refers to all those who are known as or who call themselves Christians in India. Thomas (1974:14) has noted that they form a distinct religious and social group, insofar as they consider themselves, and are considered by others, as followers of one religion, namely, Christianity. Nevertheless, Christian Indians do not form a solidary ethno-religious group. There are vast differences, not only in history, but also in doctrine, organization, practices, caste and socio-economic levels among the various Christian religious communities.

In pre-independence India, the majority of Christians scattered throughout the Indian sub-continent were lower caste and class groups who, under British rule, had embraced Christianity as a means of cultural, social and religious liberation. The Syrian Christians of southwest India, however, were a powerful community. In Bengal, in the latter part of the nineteenth century, many educated Indians and those from higher castes formulated the concept of an Oriental Christ, became Christians, and attempted a synthesis of Hindu Indian and Christian Western traditions in the process of reforming Indian cultural, religious and social structures (Thomas, 1979:54). In post-independence India, the proportion of Christians in the total population has remained fairly constant around 2.5%, the 1971 figure being 2.6% (Pendse, 1984:38).

The revival of Oriental studies; contact with Western ideas, scholars and Christian missionaries; the introduction of British education were all significant factors contributing to a changed Hindu consciousness, to the search for a new cultural and spiritual identity, to the emergence of a number of diverse Hindu reform movements, and to the rise of nationalism in nineteenth-century India.[4] Some of these movements were concerned with reform within Hinduism. Such were the Brahmo Sabha (later called the Brahmo Samaj) of 1828, and its schismatic offshoots, the Adi (original) Brahmo Samaj (1866) and the Brahmo Samaj of India (1866), led by Rammohan Roy (1714-1833), Devendranath Tagore (1817-1905) and Keshub Chunder Sen (1838-1884), respectively (Farquhar, 1915:29-74).[5] The Brahmo Samaj was the pioneer intellectual movement in early nineteenth century India which initiated the new educated classes into enlightenment, rationalism and social and religious reform (Thomas, 1979:29). In fact, it was neither Indian Christians nor Western missionaries, but Brahmo Samajists, especially men like Keshub Chunder Sen and P. C. Moozoomdar, who first attempted an indigenous interpretation of Christ in India in the late nineteenth century (Baago, 1969:12). Keshub Chunder Sen spoke and wrote of the 'Asiatic Christ' (Moozoomdar, 1931). Moozoomdar was his disciple and also wrote of the Oriental Christ as distinct from the Western Christ introduced by missionaries. The Brahmo Samajists directly influenced Christian Indians to take up the task of indigenizing Christianity.

The term *nationalism* in the Indian socio-historical context refers to a new consciousness and world-view which were manifested in a social movement. It emerged in the context of the confrontation between Western culture and Western Christianity on the one hand, and Indian culture and Hinduism on the other. The nationalist movement revived ancient traditions, emphasized Indian identity, and sought independence in all aspects of political and social life. In particular, it was a protest movement against British colonial domination and the claims of Western superiority in race, culture and religion (Thomas, 1979:14).

The early Hindu reform movements expressed an openness to Western and Christian ideas and culture as well as a revival of the Indian religious and philosophical tradition. Thomas (1979:47) has argued that contact with Christianity and the West provoked a crisis of identity among Indians: "Christianity for Indians was repulsive because it seemed to be part and parcel of the Western colonial enterprise; it was at the same time attractive to them, because it ... created in them a spiritual restlessness and the search for a new identity, the seeds of Indian nationalism." In response to the growing cultural imperialism of the British Raj, particularly with respect to the anglicization and westernization of Indian education (Thomas, 1979:48), other leaders and movements asserted their nationalism by proclaiming the superior spirituality of Indian culture and religion as compared to the materialism of Western society.

Some reform movements were explicitly protest movements. Such was the Arya Samaj, a militant religious nationalist movement founded in 1875 by Dayananda Saraswati (1824-83). Dayananda Saraswati, in opposition to the foreign religions of Islam and Christianity and to Hindu sectarianism, led a conservative movement of return to the Vedic tradition as the sole source of truth and, at the same time, of radical social reform in education, social uplift and social service. The Arya Samaj movement became institutionalized as it expanded throughout and beyond India. It was intensely nationalistic and an important factor in the growth of nationalism, especially in the Punjab. It was at the centre of communal conflicts and violence between Hindus and Muslims prior to independence; it continues to be identified occasionally with conflict between Hindus and Sikhs in contemporary India.

The early twentieth century saw the emergence in Bengal of several Neo-Hindu reform movements whose leaders and followers stimulated the revival of the ashram mode of life. Among them were Sri Ramakrishna Paramahansa (1836-86) and his disciple, Narendranath Datta, Swämi Vivekänanda (1862-1902), who, in 1897, founded the Ramakrishna Order (Math and Mission), the most important and enduring movement of reformed Hinduism.[6] Rabindranath Tagore (1861-1941) developed *Säntiniketan* ashram in 1901 from the 1863 ashram of his father, Devendranath Tagore. Another Bengali, Sri Aurobindo Ghose (1872-1950), erstwhile revolutionary nationalist, retired from politics in 1910 to settle in French Pondicherry. There he developed his system of integral yoga for the transformation of human life, gathered followers, and, in 1926, officially founded *Sri Aurobindo* ashram, which flourishes today.

Mahatma Gandhi (1869-1948) and his follower, Vinoba Bhave (1895-1981), gave a religio-political focus to the Hindu ashram tradition. Gandhi founded *Satyägraha* ashram in the village of Kochrab, near Ahmedabad, Gujarat, in May 1915, a few months after his return to India; the ashram was moved to Sabarmati in 1918.[7] The name of the ashram, *Satyägraha,* meaning the force that is born of truth and love, conveyed both the goal and the method of service of the ashram (Gandhi, 1929:334-8). Gandhi presented a proposal to his followers which was at once an order for action and an offer of *moksa* or liberation (Mühlmann, 1977:850). The rules and regulations of the draft constitution proclaimed the object of the ashram: "to learn how to serve the motherland and to serve it." In other words, the ashram was a training centre for political and social reformers. In Gandhi's view, "politics, economic progress, etc., are not considered to be independent branches of learning, but...they are all rooted in religion" (Gandhi, 1922: Appendix,5-9).

Gandhi's ashrams were based on the *Bhagavad Gītā's* doctrine of selfless service and its stress on the possibility of combining all *märgas,* or paths to salvation. Gandhi respected popular religion as much as Vedantic religion. Ashrams were not merely centres of meditation (Chatterjee, 1983:57); they were the means for learning "spiritual disciplines which provided the energy and drive for *Satyägraha* campaigns" (Pyarelal, 1958:797). Gandhi (1951:30) insisted that spiritual values should be the basis of all action. His ashram was a religious community, open to men, women and children, of any caste or none, and run according to his monastic rule. The ashramites led a life of *karma yoga* (selfless action), vowed to truth, *ahimsā* (non-violence), celibacy, control of the palate, non-stealing and non-possession. They were committed to the observance of fearlessness and *swadeshi* (the use of simple, Indian-made goods). Gandhi's ashrams were communities which stressed the dignity of manual work ('bread labour'). Common activities included menial tasks, like scavenging, which were the traditional occupation of the Untouchables. The ashramites learned to weave, and thus gave birth to the *khadi* (home-spun cloth) movement. Gandhi himself began to wear the *khadi dhoti* (cotton loin-cloth) at this time (Gandhi, 1929:555-63).

For Gandhi (1951:21), spinning and weaving were "not only the very symbol of passive resistance,...but also a means of meditation.... Every act," he said, "has its spiritual, economic and social implications." C. F. Andrews wrote to Rabindranath Tagore that Gandhi was "a saint of action rather than of contemplation" (quoted in Chatterjee, 1983:1). As Chatterjee (1983:57) has so succinctly observed, "Gandhi discovered in Hinduism a *non-contemplative* activist strand which he strengthened till it was capable of being a lifeline for the toiling millions of his country." As for his creation of ashrams, Pyarelal (1971:21) notes that Gandhiji[8] not only revived the ashrams of ancient India, "finding in them the vehicle for translating his vision of Sarvodaya society, ..." but he also "gave a new content and meaning to the *āshramas* by developing them in villages or towns right in the midst of the people, as against their being away from the people."

Gandhi refused to accept the role of *guru*. Despite his disclaimer, he clearly exercised charismatic authority in constructing an ashram with a strict communal *sādhanā* . He applied the same principles at *Sevāgrām*, the ashram he later founded near Wardha, Maharashtra, and where he settled in 1933. The ancient institution of *āsramas* was revived and reconstituted to meet the new purposes of the awakened national consciousness. When the ashram had fulfilled its purpose, he disbanded the community.

Vinoba Bhave was a follower of Gandhiji from 1916, the earliest days of *Satyāgraha* ashram.[9] In 1921, Gandhi gave Vinoba Bhave responsibility for the ashram at Wardha. For a period of twenty years or more (when he was not in jail for his part in the independence movement), Vinoba conducted various experiments in spinning, weaving, basic education, cultivation, cow-service, leper-service and other social activities. In particular, he made significant contributions to the development of *khadi* in village industries. His many jail terms provided opportunities to engage in meditation, reflection and creative writing, which were integral elements of *Sevāgrām* ashram life.

Vinoba Bhave became a *guru* in his own right. After independence, and the assassination of Gandhi, he moved out of the ashram to travel throughout India on a campaign of economic reconstruction. Like Gandhi, he believed that seekers of spiritual knowledge and liberation must also be concerned with social reconstruction. In 1951, in opposition to independent India's First Five Year Plan (for economic development), he initiated the *bhoodan* movement, which marched throughout India for about twenty-five years, seeking donation of fields and money to the landless poor as a means of self-realization. In 1952, he initiated the *gramdan* movement whereby villagers pooled their land and reorganized village life along co-operative lines. The *bhoodan* movement has been criticized by some for being a *counter*-movement to the people's movement of seizing land that they considered their right; Vinoba's preference for *bhoodan* has been attributed to his commitment to Gandhi's principle of *ahimsā* (non-violence).[10] The reconstruction of village society according to *gramdan* was a practical application of Gandhiji's principles of village self-reliance *(swāraj)* and *sarvodaya*, that is, the welfare of all based on a redistribution of wealth. From the *bhoodan* movement and the march throughout India emerged six ashrams, among them the contemporary *Brahma Vidyā Mandir* ashram at Paunar, near Wardha, Maharashtra, an ashram of women disciples who had accompanied Vinoba Bhave in his march, some of them for as long as twelve years. The expectation was that these ashrams would pursue a *sādhanā* of true spiritual knowledge *(Brahma vidyā)* which was society-oriented.

Vinoba Bhave was specifically concerned with women's liberation, both spiritual and social. His inspiration, teachings and example gave shape and substance to the *Stree Shakti Jagaran* women's movement, which has now spread beyond India. The movement is concerned with awakening of women's power to contribute toward national unity, world peace and a non-violent society. The members of *Brahma Vidyā Mandir* ashram are deeply involved in the movement.[11] Vinoba Bhave's life project was non-violent social change.

Conclusion

All of these Hindu ashram movements were identified with charismatic leaders whose authority rested on the credibility of the message they articulated in a changed socio-economic, political and cultural context. They attracted followers and gave direction to segments of Indian society who were already seeking liberation from the colonial structures of pre-independence India and from the social and cultural contradictions of post-independence India. In the relationship between the *guru* and the followers, each ashram was constructed as an appropriate indigenous Indian mode of living out the content of the *guru's* message. The ashram was a conscious expression of intense nationalism. Since independence, the movement to revive traditional Hindu ashrams has become institutionalized in the stable stuctures of large organizations. The ashram founders continue to be symbolic *gurus* for their followers today.

The heightened nationalist consciousness and the new religious movements of early twentieth-century Hinduism had a direct impact on the Christian ashram movement. Christian Indians were associated with the Neo-Hindu reform movements and with the nationalist movement. The Hindu ashram movement presented a model of indigenous organization for Christian Indians who were seeking alternative structural and cultural expressions of Christianity. In the next chapter, I will look more closely at the relationships between Hindu revivalism, nationalism and the emergence of the Christian ashram movement.

Notes

[1]Mandelbaum (1970), Schermerhorn (1978), Mundadan (1984b) and the Catholic Bishops Conference of India (1969) present good summary accounts of the history of Christianity in India. A six-volume history of Christianity in India, of which only two volumes (1983, 1984) have appeared so far, is being published by the Church History Association of India. This is an ecumenical publication which presents the history from the perspective of Christian Indians. Mundadan (1984a) produced volume 1.

[2]A notable exception was the Italian Jesuit missionary, Roberto de Nobili, who, in the first half of the seventeenth century, adopted the identity and life-style of the

sannyāsi, the Hindu celibate ascetic, learned Sanskrit, Tamil and Telugu, and studied the Vedānta to carry out his missionary activity in southern India. De Nobili's assumption was that large-scale conversions would follow from the conversion of brahmins, the members of the highest caste in society. His aim was linguistic and cultural integration (Cronin, 1959; Hambye, 1973). According to Abhishiktānanda (1959:78), de Nobili sowed the seed of Christian *sannyāsa,* that is, a consecrated life of renunciation in an Indian style and garb.

[3]Harrison (1961:405) notes that the English appointed ministers to their trading settlements, which were known as factories, but did little to promote conversion among Indians. The Society for Promoting Christian Knowledge (S.P.C.K.) was formed in London in 1699 and the Society for the Propagation of the Gospel in Foreign Parts (S.P.G.) in 1701. The trading companies were not in favour of an attack on Asiatic religions, for it would spell loss of trade (Harrison, 1961:403). The Danish missionaries, on the other hand, were not only interested in ministering to their factory and garrison, but also in conversion and direct evangelization. When the Danes acquired Serampore in Bengal in 1755, the Danish missionaries also moved there.

[4]Das (1974:vii) writes that "A spirit of inquiry, a search for a new identity as a nation and a desire to make a synthesis between the values of India and Europe--are the three cardinal features of the so-called 'Bengal Renaissance.'" Das makes the point that religion was never an isolated element of Indian society; hence, the new religious movements were not confined to theological reconstructions but also attempted to redefine social values.

[5]Under Rammohan Roy's leadership, the Brahmo Samaj had close ties with the Unitarian movement. Rammohan Roy's followers were among the upper-caste (brahmin) urban educated Hindus and were committed to a monotheistic and Upanishadic Hinduism, in opposition to Hindu sectarianism, on the one hand, and British evangelical Christian education, on the other. Divisions arose over the direction the movement would take. Under Debendranath Tagore's leadership, the monotheistic theology and the Upanishadic tradition and ethical norms of Brahmo Samaj teachings were codified; the movement was rejuvenated and reorganized, and membership grew among the secularized urban educated elite who had fallen away from sectarian devotional Hinduism *(Vaisnava bhakti)* and brahmin caste practices. Keshub Chunder Sen led a split in the Brahmo Samaj movement which also focussed on religous reform, but which stressed social and political reform; in particular, the abolition of caste distinction, the education of women, the alleviation of poverty, and a new national identity. The movement under Sen was missionary in its activities, seeking followers among all castes, beyond Bengal throughout India (hence its changed name), and even outside India. He founded the Church of the New Dispensation in 1881 (Farquhar, 1915:56) and declared himself the leader of a new universal religion which was to be the synthesis of all religions (Sen, 1938).

[6]Useful references are Williams (1981) and Singh (1983). The visit of Swāmi Vivekānanda to the World Parliament of Religions in Chicago in 1893 not only

introduced Hinduism to North America, but it also heightened Indian nationalist consciousness.

[7]I visited *Satyāgraha* ashram, Sabarmati, 6 March, 1985, and Gandhi's later ashram, *Sevāgrām,* near Wardha, 10 November, 1983. Both ashrams are now museums to Gandhiji's memory and to his principles of ashram life and political action.

[8]The suffix *-ji* added to a name denotes respect for the person. Ashram members (and many other Indians) invariably refer to Mahatma Gandhi as Gandhiji. In a similar manner, women in ashrams are referred to as Mātāji, the term *Mātā* meaning Mother. Hence, women who are leaders of ashrams are often called "The Mother."

[9]Shah's (1979) study of Vinoba Bhave's life and work, prepared for an international women's conference at *Brahma Vidyā Mandir* ashram in December 1979, not long before Vinoba's death, is a useful source of reference material.

[10]Conversation with Samuel Rayan, S.J., Vidyajyoti Institute of Religious Studies, Delhi, 4 November, 1984.

[11]I attended the *Vishwa Mahila Sammelan* International Women's Conference at *Brahma Vidyā Mandir* ashram, Paunar, Maharashtra, 9-11 November, 1983. About six hundred women attended the conference. Its stated objectives were: (1) to develop fearlessness based on awareness of inner strength and solidarity; (2) to foster mutual encouragement and enlightenment; (3) to develop understanding and a network of understanding across all barriers of culture and race; and (4) to agree upon a definite project for action as a token of our determination to work for a more just society. Conference posters proclaimed Vinoba Bhave's sayings, such as the following: "May your Spirits concur. May your Hearts concur. May your Minds work in concurrence--So that your united energies may be best organised."

CHAPTER 4

THE ASHRAM MOVEMENT:

EMERGENCE, LEADERSHIP
AND IDEOLOGY

Against this historico-social background, the ashram movement, as it is called
in the literature (Jones, 1939:200-37; Keithahn, 1973:35; Clarke, 1980:8-9; Victor,
1981:5-6; Vandana, 1983:179), emerged at the turn of this century. The leaders of
the movement all shared a common goal; namely, a new institutionalized

indigenization of Christianity (Winslow, 1929:3-5; 1930:12-7; 1954:78-9; Jesudason, 1938:202; Monchanin and Le Saux, 1951:28-9; Mattam, 1974:145-7). Protestants, Catholics and Orthodox Syrians among these leaders tended to draw their inspiration from different aspects of Hinduism. The Protestant ashram leaders were strongly influenced by the Neo-Hindu reform movements and their emphasis on social, educational, medical and health programmes and activities; for the Protestants, indigenization meant a radical stance against foreign colonial influence. The Catholic and Orthodox-Syrian leaders looked for an integration of Christian monasticism with the Hindu tradition of renunciation; for the Catholics, indigenization meant the expression of the Christian religious experience in a theology, spirituality, liturgy and symbols which were rooted in Indian culture. All the Christian leaders, however, drew from the tradition of ancient Hinduism in their conception of ashrams as an appropriate mode of Christian community organization (Jesudason, 1938; Winslow, 1954:78; Griffiths, 1974:194; 1982:23-4). As their awareness and understanding of Hinduism grew, their goals became more sharply defined to include a mutual enrichment of Hinduism and Christianity through the integration of the Hindu and Christian experience of God (Jones, 1928; Abhishiktānanda, 1969a).

The charismatic leaders of the ashram movement gave voice to the sentiments of those Christians who were concerned about the alien and unintelligible nature of the Christian message for Indians, the inadequacy of foreign institutions for the further growth of Christianity in India, and the inequality of relationships between Indians and Westerners in Christian missions.

The Protestant ashram movement

In its origins, the Protestant ashram movement was strongly influenced by the nationalist movement. Many of the leaders, such as Savarirayan Jesudason and E. Forrester Paton of *Christukula* ashram, Jack Winslow of *Christa Prema Seva Sangh* ashram, K. K. Chandy of *Christavashram* and E. Stanley Jones of *Sat Tal* ashram, based their communities on Gandhi's principles of ashram life. The founders of *Christukula* ashram, which is usually described as the first Christian ashram, consciously identified with Gandhi's *swadeshi* (use of local resources) movement at a time when this act was a political statement. Winslow and his companions visited Gandhi's *Satyāgraha* ashram, Gujarat, in 1928 (Elwin, 1964:42); other ashram leaders spent a period of time at *Satyāgraha,* or at *Sevāgrām*, Gandhi's later ashram near Wardha, Maharashtra. And Gandhiji, in turn, stayed at *Christukula* ashram (Savarirayan, 1981:46), and visited *Christa Prema Seva Sangh* ashram (Grant, 1972:542). Many Christian Indians were responsive to Gandhi's message of liberation, based on the principle of non-violence *(ahimsā)*, and his attempts to synthesize religion and politics.

The Christian ashram movement found its intellectual basis in what came to be known as the Indian Christianity movement. Nineteenth-century Oriental scholars, like Max Müller at Oxford, had aroused interest in the study of comparative religions and fostered a change of attitude toward Hinduism among Christians, both Indian and European. Under the impact of the Bengal Renaissance (as the revival movement was called), a new movement toward indigenous theological thinking began among Protestant Christian Indians. People like Krishna Mohan Bannerjea (1813-1881), as well as some Western missionaries, began the process of "rethinking Christianity in India" (Philip, 1982:1). In particular, the heavy reliance of the Orientalists on the Sanskritic tradition tended to emphasize the idyllic traditional Indian socio-religious culture. In the context of the Hindu Renaissance and the awakened nationalist consciousness, Christian Indians in the latter half of the nineteenth century began to protest against the domination and injustice of foreign missionary societies vis-à-vis Indians. The Indian Christianity movement sought to change institutionalized Christianity in India from its Western cultural forms and dominant Western missionary leadership to an indigenous institutionalized Christianity with Indian Christian leadership. Indian Christian associations were formed throughout India, and attempts were made to found a National Church: the National Church of India, led by Pulney Andy, in Madras in 1886; and the *Christo Samaj* in Calcutta in 1887, under the leadership of Kali Charan Banurji. The earliest indigenous missionary organization was the Mar Thoma Syrian Christian Evangelistic Association founded in Travancore in 1888.

It is important to note that the movement to form a National Church developed in the context of the political nationalist movement, the emergence of the freedom movement, the founding of the political nationalist Indian Association in 1876 and of the Indian National Congress in 1885. Many Christian Indians (including the leader of the National Church of Calcutta) were active participants in the Indian National Congress (Thomas, 1979:88-92). The national church movement clearly indicated that Christian Indians shared in the awakened nationalist consciousness and were part of the nationalist movement (Thomas, 1979:81-2).

The Indian Christianity movement developed various other structures to express the changed consciousness and ideologies. The National Missionary Society, an inter-denominational organization founded in 1905 on the principles of Indian leadership, Indian methods and Indian money, was an important organization in the emergence of the Christian ashram movement.[1] The first proposal for Protestant ashrams was made at the 1912 meeting of the National Missionary Society. C. F. Andrews, intimate friend and collaborator with Gandhi, made the suggestion that there was a great future for Christian ashrams (Chaturvedi and Sykes, 1949:74). Kanakarajan T. Paul, then General Secretary of the National Missionary Society, proposed that ashrams could be training centres for fulfilling both evangelical and social goals (Philip, 1946:265; Taylor, 1979:283-4). Paul's conception of a Christian ashram had much in common with Mahatma Gandhi's *Satyāgraha* ashram. Paul saw the ashram as training youth in spirituality, in evangelism and in methods of providing medical aid and of developing self-reliance among workers. M. M. Thomas (1969:281) has noted that most of the Christian ashrams which were in the forefront of inidigenization of Christianity and of Christian national service in villages were linked to the National Missionary Society.

While Gandhi was establishing *Satyāgraha* ashram in Gujarat, the great Mahararashtran poet, Narayan Vaman Tilak (1862-1919), a Hindu convert to Christianity, was pioneering a different kind of Christian ashram. In 1917, after twenty years in service of the American Marathi Mission, Tilak, at the age of fifty-five, together with his wife, adopted the life of a Hindu *sannyāsi,* or renouncer. In a public announcement he outlined his ideal. It was not to be a life of solitary meditation, but rather one in which he continued his literary activities and created an Indian-style community of service. To this end he founded an association which he called "Darbar of the Lord Jesus Christ." The aim of the Darbar was to unite baptized and unbaptized disciples of Christ, who was regarded as the Supreme Guru. Tilak's home became the ashram. The members were to engage in *nishkama karma,* or loving service without attachment to the fruits of action, as taught in the Gītā. Tilak, as founder, became chief servant of the Darbar. He gathered some forty to fifty members, who were almost all baptized Christians. His hopes for extending the Darbar among Hindus were disappointed (Winslow, 1923:121-6; Jacob, 1979:1-6,53-7).

Tilak's ashram ideal had little time for trial, for he died within twenty months of founding the Darbar. Nevertheless, his inspiration influenced an Anglican priest, Jack Winslow, who translated much of Tilak's poetry and wrote his biography. Winslow's (1923:126) comment on the Darbar was, "If it failed, it was a splendid failure; and it will not have failed if it supplies an inspiration and points a way which others may follow." Winslow makes no claim, however, that Tilak directly influenced him to found an ashram. He dates the inspiration to his reading about ancient Hindu ashrams while on home leave in 1919 (Winslow, 1954:78). On his return to India in 1920, Winslow shared his ideas with Savarirayan Jesudason, a Christian Indian, and E. Forrester Paton, a Scot, both medical doctors with a similar vision of an indigenized Christianity. These three men became the founders of ashrams which persist today.

In 1921, Winslow (1954:79-88) gathered a following of Christian Indians who formed a community, which was called *Christa Seva Sangha.* The community had no settled home for four years, but moved around Ahmednagar district, until, in 1927, Winslow established an ashram, called *Christa Seva Sangha,* in Pune, for a small group of Christian Indians and some English Christians who came to join them. Among them was the renowned anthropologist, Verrier Elwin, who became an ardent follower of Gandhi, and who in 1930 mobilized the ashram into direct political action in Gandhi's support, to the consternation of the established Church of India (Elwin, 1964:47-9).

In structuring ashram life, Tilak and Winslow also drew from the *bhakti* (devotional) tradition of Hinduism. Christian Indian poets of South India, like Tilak and H. A. Krishna Pillai (1827-1900), composed lyrics which expressed in indigenous language and imagery the *bhaktā's* desire for union with a personal God (Boyd, 1969:110-18). Winslow adopted these lyrics, accompanied by Indian music, for worship in *Christa Seva Sangha* ashram, and urged that an Indian Christian theology, which took cognizance of the devotional tradition, be developed

(Winslow, 1958:43-52). *Bhakti* was one of the principal modes of service for *Christa Seva Sangha* ashram (Winslow, 1928:11).

Winslow (1926) made a study of the mystical intuition of India, particularly in three of its most characteristic expressions: *bhakti-mārga* (the way of devotion), *sannyāsa* (the way of renunciation), and *yoga* (the way of discipline). Winslow worked out Farquhar's suggestion that Christianity could fulfil the ascetic tendencies in Hinduism by combining a life of austerity and contemplation with service to community (Webb, 1981:41). Chakkarai was deeply aware also of the mystical experience in Hinduism; he argued that an indigenization of Christianity must integrate the Indian religious consciousness with Christian faith and experience. Thomas (1981:11,31) has stated the case for such an integration as follows: The mystical consciousness of the *Christian bhaktā* will be expressed by devotion to the Lord Jesus.

Meanwhile, Jesudason and Forrester Paton, in 1921, established the first major Protestant ashram, *Christukula* (the Family of Christ), at Tirupattur, in Tamil Nadu, about two hundred and twenty-five kilometres south-west of Madras. They affiliated the ashram with the National Missionary Society, and also consciously identified with the Gandhian *swadeshi* movement. Both were concerned with the adoption of indigenous modes of evangelism and with the provision of medical and other social services (Savarirayan, 1981:7-9).

In the early twentieth century, a number of Christian Indian writers began to express Christian theology in terms of Indian thought forms (Lalchhuanliana, 1973:127-34). Among them, the Madras Rethinking Christianity Group, which was formed in the1930s, was an important voice for the new outlook. The members of the group were all ardent nationalists.[2] Several of them were members of an association called the Bangalore Conference Continuation, which met, in 1917 and for several years thereafter, in cities of South India. Its purpose was to discuss religious, social, economic and political issues of the country and to prepare the church for radical transformation in outlook and policy, so that it would carry out its mission in the contemporary national situation (Lalchhuanliana, 1973:88-91). The group expressed its views in two periodicals, *The Christian Patriot* and *The Guardian,* and in a book, *Rethinking Christianity in India* (Devasahayam and Sudarisanam, 1938). They explicitly argued the case for the Protestant ashram movement, claiming that ashrams were an appropriate model for Christian community organization in India. Chakkarai (1938:115) saw ashrams as communities "for the deepening of spiritual life apart from the bigger (church) organisation." Jesudason (1937;1938:215-24) and Chenchiah, Chakkarai and Sudarisanam (1941) all wrote detailed studies of the origin, nature and development of Hindu and Christian ashrams.

The changed religious consciousness and ideological perspective were also reflected in the speeches and writings of some Western Protestant missionaries and theologians, like William Miller and A. C. Hogg of Madras Christian College; C. F. Andrews of St. Stephen's College;[3] J. N. Farquhar of Oxford;[4] and E. Stanley Jones, the American Methodist missionary; all of whom were sympathetic to the Indian perspective on Indian Christianity.

In addition, E. Stanley Jones, in the 1920s, began a process of inter-religious dialogue among Hindus, Christians, Buddhists and Sikhs in meetings which he called Round Table Conferences. Such gatherings not only reflected the changed consciousness; they also provided a context for sharing goals and experiences. At the same time, they fostered the development of ashrams, such as the one founded by Jones at Sat Tal in 1930, which were concerned about breaking the lines between the colonizer and the colonized (Jones,1932; Taylor, 1973).

Movements such as the Indian Christianity movement, the national church movement, the Madras Rethinking Christianity Group and the Christian ashram movement can be described in Traugott's (1978) terminology as *extra*-institutional in their orientation; that is, they were attempts by minority groups of the institutional Christian churches to develop strategies, to formulate an ideology (theology), and to mobilize support for alternative institutional structures and processes. They were not *anti*-institutional in their orientation.

Just as the nineteenth-century Indian Christianity movement provoked a counter-movement among Western missionaries and the foreign missionary societies, so too the twentieth-century movement among intellectuals and writers met strong opposition from the same sources. The foreign missionaries, for the most part, were anti-nationalist in their sentiments (Boyd, 1969:86). Nevertheless, the Indian Christianity movement mobilized some support from the church at large. The World Missionary Conference, held at Tambaram, Madras, in 1939, inspired by C. F. Andrews and ashram leaders, gave support to the ashram movement as an experiment for the enrichment of Christian community life (International Missionary Council, 1938:8; Jesudason, 1940:150).

The foundation of the Christian Institute for the Study of Religion and Society in 1957, under the auspices of the National Christian Council of India, with P. D. Devanandam as its first director, continued the process in post-independence India of developing an indigenous Christian theology and an awakened socio-religious consciousness (Taylor, 1983).   In particular, Devanandam promoted dialogue between Christians and non-Christians, especially Hindus (Boyd, 1969:202). Under Devanandam, and his successors as director, M. M. Thomas and S. K. Chatterji, the Institute has done much to foster the development of Indian Christian theology and to stimulate research into social, economic and political change.   In the last ten years, it has moved toward studies of the very poor, harijans, tribals and women, and toward seeking resources for oppressed groups (Taylor, 1983:260-62).

The Catholic ashram movement

In pre-independence India, Syrian Christians and Roman Catholics, for the most part, were not identified with the nationalist movement.   They tended to isolate themselves from Indian social and political life in general, and from the nationalist and independence movements in particular (CBCI, 1969:183; Schermerhorn, 1978:194). The seeds of an indigenous form of Catholicism germinated only after the Second Vatican Council of the sixties, when India was already an independent nation.   Vatican II provided the legitimation and ideological framework for an inculturated liturgy and for the emergence of Catholic ashrams.[5]

Although the Catholic ashram movement belongs properly to the period of post-independence India, the first proposal for a Catholic ashram came at the turn of the century from a Bengali brahmin, Bhavani Charan Banerji, a convert to Christianity in 1891.   Before his conversion he was closely associated with the Brahmo Samajists. He became a member of the Church of the New Dispensation, with its founder, Keshub Chunder Sen, as his guru (Animānanda, 1947:31).   He was also influenced by his association with Dayananda Saraswati, the leader of the Arya Samaj Hindu reform movement, particularly in his strong emphasis on the

Vedas. Apparently a colourful and somewhat erratic personality, Brahmabandhab Upadhyay, as he chose to be called after his conversion to Christianity, expounded in lectures and writings (particularly in a monthly journal called *Sophia*) the ideas that became the foundation of the Christian ashram movement. Brahmabandhab Upadhyay (1896:15-6) donned the ochre-coloured robe of a renunciate, or *sannyāsi*, and, together with Swāmi Animānanda, another Hindu convert to Catholicism, worked for the foundation of a monastery, *Kasthalika Matha*, an institution through which he attempted to integrate the spirit of ancient Christian monasticism with the traditional structures and ascetic life-styles of Hindu ashrams.[6] Despite initial episcopal support, Brahmabandhab Upadhyay's experimental *math* met with incomprehension and opposition, and it had to be abandoned after a few months. Brahmabandhab Upadhyay remained a Catholic and a fiery nationalist. He played a significant role in the *swadeshi* movement, and he was also a follower of Rabindranath Tagore's movement for national education in the early part of this century.

The Catholic ashram movement found its ideological base in the work of some foreign missionaries and scholars who shared the changed attitude toward Hinduism and who, in their turn, had been influenced by the ideas and writings of Brahmabhandab Upadhyay. Two Belgian theologians and philosophers, C. Dandoy and P. Johanns, in collaboration with Swāmi Animānanda, Brahmabandhab Upadhyay's disciple, produced a monthly journal, *The Light of the East*, in the 1920s and 1930s. The aim of the journal was explicitly missionary. The articles were "primarily intended for Hindus, Parsis, Mohammedans, Jains, Buddhists and others," but also for Indian Christian priests, that they might understand non-Christian religions (Johanns, 1930, IX:1). The journal, therefore, was an important source of ideas and philosophy for a small minority of Catholics who were interested in indigenization of Christianity. In a series of one hundred and thirty-seven articles, over a period of twelve years, Johanns (1922-1934:I,3-XII,7) systematically developed the thesis that if the disconnected statements of the Vedāntic philosophers were to be brought into harmony in a system, that system would be akin to Thomism (1922:1,3). Johanns' goal in the articles was to provide a synthesis of the Vedāntic systems of philosophy, and thus to demonstrate the fulfilment of Hinduism in Christianity.

Mattam (1974, 1975) has made a study of several Catholic pioneers of an indigenized Christianity. Besides Johanns, he has singled out Olivier Lacombe, a French scholar of Hinduism; Jacques-Albert Cuttat, a Swiss diplomat and scholar of Oriental spirituality; Robert Charles Zaehner, an English professor of Eastern religions and ethics; and Abbé Jules Monchanin, the French priest and scholar, who was an active participant in the Madras Cultural Academy.

According to Mattam's (1975:44-68) analysis, Lacombe considered that the meeting of Christianity and Hinduism was possible only at a level beyond and beneath systems of belief and expressions of religious experience. Lacombe was concerned with the nature of Hindu mystical experience and its relation to Christian mystical experience. For Lacombe, the dialogue between Hindu and Christian would be at the level of religious experience itself. The meeting-point between Hindu and Christian would be in the Absolute.

Cuttat (1957, 1967, 1969) studied the history of the encounter of Eastern and Western spiritualities. He argued that the better the Christian understood his or her own religion, the better he or she would understand that of others from within; and, inversely, the better Christians understood an alien religion from within, the more likely they were to deepen understanding of their own faith. Cuttat (1962:57-65) maintained that the common spiritual basis of Christian and Asiatic religions is "consciousness of the sacred." For him, this awareness is the indispensable condition of spiritual encounter of East and West. He argued for a new spiritual approach to the world, and he recommended Ramakrishna, Vivekānanda, Aurobindo and Rabindranath Tagore as exemplars of this approach. He was, in other words, significantly attuned to and influenced by the Neo-Hindu reform movements of the early twentieth century. Cuttat, together with Swāmi Abhishiktānanda and the Reverend C. Murray Rogers, was one of the founders of a "circle" of Christians who regularly engaged in "internal dialogue" about the encounter of Christian and non-Christian religions, as preparation for "external dialogue" with non-Christians (Rogers, 1965:35-44).

Zaehner insisted on the differences between Hinduism and Christianity (Mattam, 1975:111-43). Nevertheless, Zaehner argued for a Christian approach to Hinduism which focussed on the sacred scriptures and noted what was common to

Hinduism and Christianity. According to Zaehner, "mysticism is the privileged field of encounter with Hinduism" (Mattam, 1975:135). Monchanin was a brilliant French scholar with a deep love of India. His life goal was the total Christianisation of India through an Indianisation of Christianity (Mattam, 1975:144-6). He envisaged the foundation of Christian ashrams as the means to this goal. Monchanin was convinced that contemplative monastic life, expressed in Indian form, was the appropriate mode for assimilating the rich spiritual heritage of India and for fulfilling India's quest for the Absolute. In his lectures and writings for future missionaries, Monchanin (1974) presented a radically new contemplative vision of mission which sought to uncover the ways of the Spirit in the unfolding of Indian cultural and religious history. In order to realize this conviction, Monchanin came to India in 1939 as a diocesan priest and a member of the Society of Auxiliaries of the Missions. He conceived of India as the "Land of the Trinity;" hence, the ashram he founded was dedicated to the Holy Trinity. For Monchanin, Indian spirituality would be transfigured in the Trinity, and Indian mysticism would infuse a new life within Christianity (Weber, 1969:81). Monchanin found a forum for expounding his ideas in scholarly contexts, such as the Madras Cultural Academy. In one such gathering, he discussed the quest of the Absolute in Hindu mysticism (Monchanin, 1957:46-51). He outlined the three classical ways *(karma-mārga, bhakti-mārga* and *jñāna-mārga)* open to the Hindu seeker, and then proceeded to argue that *jñāna-mārga,* the way seemingly most removed from Christianity, is a single-minded mystical quest of the Absolute which resonates with Christian mysticism.

The intellectual and spiritual basis of Catholic ashrams lies, first, in the ideas and writings of such scholars; and secondly, in the process of inter-religious dialogue, reflection and meditation, which they initiated. The shared understanding of Christian and Hindu sacred books (the Bible and the Upanishads, respectively), of Hindu and Christian philosophy, and of religious experience provided a base for clarifying the goals and structure of Christian ashrams. They encouraged the adoption of Hindu symbolism in Christian worship (Abhishiktānanda, 1968-69). The assumption was that an indigenous theology would spring from indigenous liturgy and Indian spirituality, especially under its mystical aspect (Smart, 1968; Amalorpavadass, 1980:279-82).

In 1950, Monchanin, together with a French Benedictine monk, Dom Henri Le Saux, founded the first Catholic ashram, *Saccidānanda* ashram, *Shāntivanam*, at Kulittalai, on the banks of the sacred Kavery river in Tamil Nadu (Monchanin and Le Saux, 1951). They later took the names Swāmi Parama Arubi Anandam and Swāmi Abhishiktānanda, respectively (Abhishiktānanda, 1959). Like the Catholic scholars who promoted an indigenized Christianity, the religious leaders who pioneered the Catholic ashram movement in post-independence India, such as Monchanin and Le Saux; Dom Bede Griffiths, who, with Father Francis Mahieu, in 1955, founded *Kurisumala* ashram in the western ghats of Kerala; were not Indian but European (French, Belgian and British). For the most part, they belonged to contemplative monastic orders, such as the Benedictines and the Cistercians. They sought an adaptation of contemplative Western monastic life to the Indian socio-religious context and an integration of Hindu and Christian spirituality. In particular, they adopted the Indian spiritual tradition of *sannyāsa* (renunciation): its scriptures, dress, life-style and customs. They initiated and encouraged scholarly exchanges and inter-religious dialogue, which were carried on with intensity and purpose in the fifties and early sixties.[7]

In his exploration of Hindu spirituality, Abhishiktānanda was a devoted student of the *Upanishads* and quite literally became a disciple at the feet of two Hindu spiritual masters, Sri Rāmana Mahārshi at the sacred mountain of Arunāchala at Tiruvannāmalai, and Sri Gñānānanda of Thapovanam ashram, Tyrukkoyilur (Abhishiktānanda, 1970a, 1974:19-40, 1979a; Davy,1981:195; Stuart, 1982:478).[8] Abhishiktānanda, like Rāmana Mahārshi, was a *jñāna-yogi* and an *advaitan* (non-dualist). He saw monasticism, whether Hindu or Christian, as one basically identical vocation.[9] Abhishiktānanda (1958:106-13) envisaged hermits and monks living in small ashrams, which would serve as centres of prayer, liturgy, study and work; and even as training-centres (*gurukula*) for priests (Abhishiktānanda, 1970b:68). Abhishiktānanda (1969a, 1969b, 1974, 1975, 1979b, 1986) committed to writing in books, letters and journals the fruits of his Christian *advaitan* experience. He became an intellectual leader and a guru among a significant minority of Catholics who favoured drawing at the source of Hindu spirituality for a renewed expression of Christianity.

Many Christian Indians, however, were so thoroughly Europeanized, or so thoroughly socialized to perceive Hinduism as paganism, that the step toward a Hindu contemplative style of life in an ashram was much greater for them than it was for the Europeans (Siauve, 1974:ix). It is only since the Second Vatican Council, which propounded the development of an indigenous theology and philosophy, that Indians have begun to take a significant place in the Catholic ashram movement.

The All-India Seminar on "The Church in India Today" (CBCI, 1969), which was held at Bangalore in May 1969, was a landmark in encouraging the development of Indian Christian theology, and, in particular, in mobilizing the Catholic ashram movement. It presented a vision of a new society, a new approach to non-Christian religions, and a new awareness of the meaning of Christian presence and the church's mission in Indian society. It focussed attention on the mystical tradition of Indian spirituality and stressed the need for ashrams as communities which would give birth to and nourish prayerful people (Grant, 1984:171). In 1976, the Catholic Bishops' Conference of India officially entrusted to its Commission for Liturgy the promotion and guidance of ashrams in India (Amalorpavadass, 1984:306). Catholic theologians, like Raimundo Panikkar (1964, 1977), Abhishiktānanda (1969a, 1969b, 1974), Griffiths (1966, 1976, 1982), and Amalorpavadass (1971, 1980), have provided a theological and ideological basis for the flowering of Catholic ashrams which has taken place in the last fifteen years.

Over a period of more than twenty years, Christian religious leaders, in dialogue among themselves and with Hindu *sannyāsis,* have deepened their knowledge of Hindu sacred writings and traditions, and have integrated this knowledge with their own religious tradition. At the same time, they have published manuscripts and systematically organized conferences, workshops and living experiences for clerics, religious men and women, and lay persons with the express purpose of communicating the message of an indigenized Catholic theology, liturgy and spirituality.

The most significant body in mobilizing and organizing the movement toward an indigenous Christianity has been the National Biblical, Catechetical and Liturgical Centre in Bangalore, established by the Catholic Bishops Conference of

India.   Under the leadership of Father D. S. Amalorpavadass, the NBCLC has taken pioneering steps in "renewal and adaptation" of the Roman Catholic church, along indigenous lines, according to Vatican II principles. Amalorpavadass, in his publications and lectures, and in the various national and international seminars which he has initiated, first, as director of the National Biblical, Catechetical and Liturgical Centre in Bangalore, then as Professor of Christianity at the University of Mysore, has been the most articulate exponent of an indigenous theology (Emprayil, 1980:93-103). He has also become, as I will show in Chapter 8, one of the most prominent leaders of the contemporary Catholic ashram movement.

Conclusion

The evidence clearly demonstrates that both the pre-independence Protestant ashram movement and the post-independence Catholic ashram movement emerged from and took shape *within* the structures of the established churches. Both movements were concerned with an Indianisation of the church whereby the foreign or Western character of Christianity had to be replaced by Indian cultural forms and religious traditions (which were usually identified as Hindu cultural forms and traditions). The leaders of the Protestant ashram movement gave voice to widely-held sentiments among Protestant Indians who sought an indigenized and Indian-controlled Christianity. They entered into dialogue with Buddhists, Sikhs and Muslims, as well as Hindus. They allied themselves with the nationalist movement, mobilized groups and resources, and formed associations which supported and spear-headed the ashram movement.

The emergence of the Catholic ashram movement followed a different pattern. Its original leaders were foreign, not Indian. They were isolated individuals who had practically no followers and a minimal ecclesiastical support. They began a process of cultural adaptation through the introduction of Indian symbols and art forms (such as images of Christ and the Virgin Mary in Indian garb), of Indian music, lyrics and dance, of Indian dress and life-style among themselves. It was the Second Vatican Council and its implementation in India (signalled by the 1969 All India Seminar) which provided the seed-bed for an awakened Catholic consciousness and a movement for Indianised liturgy and spirituality. A process of inculturation of the Catholic Church in India began. The process involves the development of an incarnational Catholic theology and spirituality which express the historically and culturally conditioned religious experience of Catholic Indians and which emphasize the need to incarnate the particular customs, rituals, values and myths of a particular local community (Drego, 1981:261). This movement began among some bishops, priests, religious men and women, rather than among laity. The promotion of Catholic ashrams is under the *aegis* of the Liturgical Commission of the Catholic Bishops Conference of India. Any formation of ashrams and any 'experimentation' in inculturated liturgy and symbols has to be approved by the Catholic Bishops Conference of India.

Notes

[1]The National Missionary Society emerged from the national church movement of the latter half of the nineteenth century. It was founded by Christian Indian nationalists in order to work explicitly for a national mission and indigenous church, independent of foreign missionary societies (Boyd, 1969:87-8; Thomas, 1969:276; Thomas, 1979:146; Taylor, 1979:283-4).

[2]The group included among its members G. V. Job, P. Chenchiah, V. Chakkarai, A. J. Appasamy, D. M. Devasahayan, S. Jesudason, Eddy Asirvatham and A. N. Sudarisanam, of whom Chakkarai was the most outspoken. Thomas (1981) has edited a volume on Chakkarai's speeches and writings.

[3]See his biography, by Chaturvedi and Sykes (1949).

[4]Farquhar's (1919) major work, *The Crown of Hinduism,* develops the thesis that Hinduism has been 'fulfilled' in Christianity, which he calls the 'crown' of Hindu thought and worship. Farquhar's numerous publications have been exhaustively analyzed and critically evaluated by Sharpe (1965). I discussed Farquhar's work with Professor Sharpe in an interview at the University of Sydney, 16 July, 1984.

[5]The documents of the Second Vatican Council of specific concern for inculturation of Christianity in India are: "The Dogmatic Constitution of the Church" *(Lumen Gentium),* "The Pastoral Constitution on the Church in the Modern World" *(Gaudium et Spes),* "The Decree on Ecumenism" *(Unitas Redingratio),* "The Decree on the Church's Missionary Activity" *(Ad Gentes),* and "The Decree on Eastern Catholic Churches" *(Orientalium Ecclesiarum).* English translations of all these documents are published by Abbott (1966).

[6]The proposal for *Kasthalika Matha* is presented in *Sophia*, vol. V (May, 1898), 78-9.

[7]Abhishiktānanda (1969a) has an excellent discussion of Hindu-Christian dialogue, based on meetings dealing with Hindu and Christian spirituality which were held at Shāntivanam in 1957, 1958 and 1960; at Almora in 1961; at Rajpur in 1962; at Delhi in 1963; at Nagpur in 1963. Kalapesi (1964:71-6) reports on the fourth meeting on Hindu and Christian spirituality at Jyotiniketan ashram, April 1964; Klostermaier (1966:72-75) describes the sixth meeting at Jyotiniketan, 17-21 January 1966. The editor of *Religion and Society* (1969,16/2:69-88) presents a Report on the joint Roman Catholic and non-Roman Catholic Consultation on the theology of Hindu-Christian Dialogue, Bombay, 4-8 January, 1969. Lederle (1984) presents a recent consideration of ashrams and dialogue.

[8]Henri Le Saux first visited Rāmana Mahārshi in January 1949 and regarded the visit as his initiation into Hindu monastic life (Abhishiktānanda, 1979a:vii-x). He visited Arunāchala and its caves several times after the foundation of *Saccidānanda* ashram, and after the death of Rāmana Mahārshi in 1950. Davy (1981) records that he spent several months there in 1952, in 1953, and again in 1954. In 1955 he met Swāmi Gñānānanda, and he stayed at Thapovanam ashram again in 1956 and in 1957.

[9]According to Stuart (1982:483), Abhishiktānanda, as a Christian, experienced non-duality in the experience of Jesus, his Lord and *Sadguru*. However, Gispert-Sauch (1976:503-4) interprets Abhishiktānanda as "coming uncomfortably close to bypassing the flesh of Jesus Christ."

CHAPTER 5

KEY HINDU CONCEPTS

Central to the construction and ideology of Christian ashrams are certain key concepts and institutions of ancient, post-Vedic and modern Hinduism. Some Christian Indians, but an even greater number of foreign scholars, monks, ordained and lay missionaries, and religious men and women studied Hindu sacred scriptures and philosophy, and Hindu institutions, rites and beliefs. Some lived in Hindu ashrams; some even became disciples of Hindu ascetics, such as Rāmana Mahārshi and Mahatma Gandhi. From their knowledge and experience, these leaders adopted various aspects of Hindu theology, philosophy and institutions which seemed appropriate to them for an indigenization of Christian communities, symbols, life-styles and practices.

At this point in the discussion, therefore, it may be helpful to identify the salient Hindu concepts and to indicate their significance for the Christian ashram movement. I single out the following for explication and elaboration: *āsrama, sannyāsa, guru, sādhanā* and *mārga*.

1. *Āsrama*. The sanskrit term *āsrama* is derived from the root *sram,* which means exertion; that is, a stage of intense exertion in the duties of life (Kane, 1941:425). Sanskrit writers, however, also describe *āsrama* as a place where *tapas* (austerities) are performed. The term *āsrama* thus has two meanings: (1) the hermitage or forest dwelling-place of a person who spends his time in meditation and austerities, and (2) the stages in the life of a twice-born Hindu, characterized by appropriate spiritual exertion (Chenchiah, 1941:3-5). The two meanings, although distinct, are related, and both have bearing on the development of Christian ashrams.

It was in the forest hermitages that the *risis* (seers) are believed to have received the *Vedas* (the *sruti,* or hearings) from the gods. There they are believed to have composed the *Upanisads* (the *Vedānta,* or end of the Vedas), which describe their experience of *Brahman* (the Impersonal Absolute, ground and source of all reality) and the *Ātman* (the soul, individual self, ground and source of all consciousness). The *Upanisads* became the source of the most important of the orthodox schools of Hindu philosophy. Sitting at the feet of the *risis* (the literal meaning of the sanskrit term *upanisad*), disciples listened to their teaching and shared their experience of *Brahman* (Parrinder, 1971:236,293,298-9). Roman Catholic ashrams, in particular, have drawn heavily on the Upanishadic tradition and Vedānta philosophy (especially non-dualist *advaita* philosophy) for their inspiration and ideology (Abhishiktānanda, 1969a; 1974; Griffiths, 1982). Leaders of the Protestant ashram movement, however, have also turned to this ancient Hindu heritage for their inspiration (Jesudason, 1937:2; Winslow, 1954:78).

The second meaning of *āsrama,* namely, the stages of life of a twice-born Hindu, also has import for Christian ashrams. From the times of the *Dharma Shāstras* (the sacred writings of Hindu customary law), the number of stages of life has been four: *brahmacārya* (student), *grihasthya* (householder), *vānaprastha* (hermit or forest-dweller), and *sannyāsin* (renouncer or ascetic). There has been some variation in *āsrama* theory, (a) as to the order of the stages; (b) as to whether a person must pass in sequence through all stages, or whether one could drop one or more stage and pass on to the next (for example, from *brahmacārya* to *sannyāsin*); and (c) as to the relative superiority of each successive stage, or, on the contrary, the superior status of the householder (Kane, 1941:424-26). Sen (1961:22) has noted that in a sense the *grihasthya* is to be considered the mainstay of the four *āsramas*, "for it gives unity and coherence to the entire social structure and the other *āsramas* depend on it for their sustenance." The idea underlying *āsrama dharma* was that life should be ordered in a continuous effort toward spiritual growth and attainment of the religious goal of *moksa* (liberation of the soul from the cycle of life and death) by steady and sure means (Gonda, 1965:311).

The Christian ashram movement adopted this notion of ashram in its emphasis on a life characterized by meditation, asceticism and strenuous spiritual endeavour in all stages or statuses of membership. The ideology describes a community of seekers of the Absolute, gathered around a spiritual guide who points the way to salvation. Ideally the members of the ashram comprise those in the *vānaprastha* stage, who have fulfilled their duties as householders and in whom "gray hairs and wrinkles have appeared" (Kane, 1941:412); together with *brahmachārins* (disciples or students). Nevertheless, just as Hinduism after the time of the Buddha developed *mathas* (monasteries) of *sannyāsins* (renouncers), primarily as centres for teachers and pupils (Kane, 1941:906-7), so too some Christian ashrams have celibate *sannyāsins* living together in community with *brahmachārins* (disciples or students).

2. *Sannyāsa*. The term *sannyāsa* refers to a life of asceticism and renunciation of all worldly ties, for contemplation of the Absolute and as preparation for final emancipation from *samsāra* (the wheel of time and birth-death-rebirth) (Kane, 1941:930). According to the *advaitic* (monist) tradition, the goal is identification with the Absolute; in the theistic tradition, the goal is union in love with a personal God (Dhavamony, 1978:40-1). The concept *sannyāsa* dates back to the earliest Upanishads. A *sannyāsin* (renouncer) typically is a brahmin who has

entered the fourth stage of *āsrama dharma*, as outlined above, and who has abandoned the world to become a mendicant (Parrinder, 1971:244). According to Kane (1941:942-3), opinion was sharply divided as to whether *sannyāsa* was allowed only to brahmins; he asserts that Sankarāchārya, the great *advaitin* philosopher of the eighth century, affirmed that only brahmins could be *sannyāsins*. Moreover, in the orthodox Hindu tradition, *sannyāsa* was open to men alone (King, 1984:71); in rare cases only, women adopted the ascetic mode of life in brahmanic times (Kane, 1941:945). Women renouncers are found in the later Yoga and Tantra traditions, as *yogini* and *bhairavi*, respectively.

According to many interpretations (Āchārya, 1970:120), *sannyāsa* is not just an extension of the the first three *āsramas* of *brahmacārya, grihasthya* and *vānaprastha*. It indicates a total break with the past, in response to an irresistible call to live beyond every state of life. Hence, at any period in life, one could withdraw from worldly pursuits, omitting the intervening stages, and assume the order of *sannyāsa* (Kane, 1941:424; Geden, 1918:730). Dumont (1957:16-7) postulates an essential dichotomy between the renouncer as an "individual-outside-the-world" in contrast to the "man-in-the-world." Dumont and Pocock (1960:38) draw attention to the central role of the institution of renunciation in Indian religion. Dumont (1957:16-7) claims that "the secret of Hinduism may be found in the dialogue between the renouncer and the man-in-the-world." On the other hand, Thapar (1981:274) suggests that "the main thrust of *āsrama* theory was to reduce the absolute dichotomy (between renouncer and man-in-the-world) by introducing an interplay of the dialectic of the householder and the renouncer in each of the *āsramas,* but with one being given greater prominence over the other." Thapar argues that the binary opposition lies "in the content of each of the four *(āsramas)* " (274). Moreover, Thapar points out that a renouncer who joined an order of *sannyāsins* was brought back into performing a social role; he was also involved in trying to change the social order. Such was the case with some of the great socio-political reformers of India, such as Gandhiji and Swāmi Vivekānanda.

Sannyāsa as a way of life has many features of asceticism which are common to all religions; such as fasting, or at least reducing the intake of food; abstention from meat, drink and pleasures of sense; life-long celibacy and total absence of sensual gratification; vow of silence; sleeping on bare ground; minimal clothing;

contempt of the world (Kane, 1941:975). Most of the duties prescribed for *sannyāsins* are practically the same as those for *vānaprasthas*. Kane (1941:928-9) notes the similarities and differences between the two orders. Both have to regulate the intake and quality of food; both have to contemplate on the passages of the *Upanisads* and strive for knowledge of Brahman. The hermit could be accompanied by his wife; the renouncer could not. The hermit lives a retired life, giving himself to the practice of spiritual exercise in a settled place; the renouncer leads a wandering life. The hermit has to keep his sacred fires and perform daily sacrifices; the renouncer gives them up. The hermit concentrates on *tapas* (austerities); while the renouncer is concerned primarily with control of the senses and contemplation of supreme Reality. Klostermaier (1968:18) observes that in modern times there is hardly any difference between the terms *vānaprastha* and *sannyāsa*. Although it was taught by the Brahmanical school that *sannyāsa* was the most sublime way of life, Kane (1941:975) claims that "it is a partial truth that Indians have the highest regard for the ascetic."

A point of controversy in the history of the Christian ashram movement has been the question of celibacy, some arguing that members could be married householders (Chakkarai, 1938:115; Chenchiah, 1941:233); others, that they should be celibate (Jesudason, 1938:222). As I have noted above, the *vānaprastha* hermit could be accompanied by his wife, whereas the *sannyāsin* could not; in the orthodox Hindu tradition, however, both had to observe celibacy (Kane, 1941:928). The itinerant life of the *sannyāsin* has been perceived by some Christians (Brahmabandha Upadhyaya, 1898:79; Neill, 1964:482, reporting on Sādhu Sundar Singh; Ittyavirah, 1970:194) as more appropriate than the life of *vānaprastha* for communicating the Gospel message and for involvement in the world. Immanuel (1950:100) observes, however, that the fourth stage of complete renunciation *(sannyāsa),* though appealing to Roman Catholic Indians, seems to elicit little response from Protestant Indians; the *vānaprastha* stage, on the other hand, does attract Protestant Indians.

3. *Guru.* The term *guru* literally means heavy, the Weighty One (Stutley, 1977:107). It signifies the belief that mighty or holy persons have a spiritual attribute which is measured in quantity. The *guru* is the one who, on account of his

or her special knowledge and function, is held to be the bearer of power, of weight and influence. The term *guru* applies not only to spiritual teachers, but also to other venerable persons, such as father, mother, king or any elderly person (Gonda, 1965:240). Hence the *guru-sisya* (disciple) relationship in Upanishadic times was not limited to formal ties between the ascetic *guru* living in the forest hermitage and the student who came to study at his feet; it applied also to the spiritual father-son relationship (Miller, 1980:84). The *guru* as spiritual guide in the Upanishadic tradition *(Advaya Taraka Up.* 14-18) is the one who dispels darkness; the one who dispels the mists of empirical knowledge and enables a person to become conscious that the world is a transitory dwelling until the time of *moksa,* or release *(Ch. Up.* 6.14.1ff); the one who is learned in the scriptures and established in Brahman *(Mund., Up.* 1.2.12).

Gonda (1965:241) also distinguishes between the functions of (a) *guru,* the one who performs the *samskāras* (sacraments) from conception to initiation, and who maintains the child and imparts the Vedas to it (originally the father); (b) *ācārya,* the one from whom the pupil gathers the knowledge of his socio-religious duties *(dharma)*; and (c) *upadhyaya,* the one who for his livelihood teaches a portion of the Veda. Gonda notes that the institution of guruship acquired the cumulative functions of imparting to the young male member of the Aryan community the sacraments of initiation *(diksā),* of teaching him a portion of the Veda, and of educating him. In the brahmanic period, the moral and intellectual formation of the disciple or religious student *(brahmachārin)* took place in the *guru's* house *(gurukula).* The *guru* was sometimes placed on a level with God *(Svetasvatar Up.* 6.23), and Gonda (1965:252) has observed that the doctrine of the "grace *(prasāda)* of the *guru,*" introduced in the *Mahābhārata,* is indicative of the increasing deification of the *guru.* Weber (1958a:319) has noted that for some Hindu sects the *guru* can be regarded as more than teacher, spiritual guide and exemplar who leads the disciple to God; he (or she) can actually become deified as a living god. For Rämana Mahärshi (1972:370), "God, Grace and Guru are all synonymous and also eternal and immanent." Hence, the *guru* can exercise tremendous power over disciples and exact strict obedience (Farquhar, 1915: 178-9).

In sociological terms, the *guru* may be described as a type of religious functionary. McMullen (1982:133) sums up the particular characteristic of the *guru* as follows: "a person who claims and is believed to possess some kind of mystical knowledge or enlightenment; who is willing to pass this knowledge or its aspects to the disciple; who possesses some degree of charismatic authority, and, more often than not, is non-conformist."

The institution of guruship was central to ancient Hinduism; first, because of the insistence on oral transmission, with great weight placed on correct pronunciation and recitation of the Veda; secondly, because of the belief in the necessity of a spiritual guide to attain knowledge of Brahman *(brahmavidyā)* and liberation *(moksa)*. The *guru,* as source of all learning, retained the supreme position in Indian culture throughout changes in Hinduism and the development of different philosophies, which gave rise to a diversity of sects and various schools of yoga. Miller (1980:85) has noted that "in medieval India the *guru* often remained a householder who functioned solely as a teacher." More commonly, however, "he was an ascetic *(sādhu)* who lived in total detachment in a forest hermitage *(āśrama)* or who resided in a large monastery *(matha)* located near a temple in an urban area." Moreover, it was during this period that the *guru-sisya* relationship became concretely expressed in the various monastic orders which had their origin in one or other of the five great historical teachers or *ācāryas,* who expounded a philosophical system and who established a monastic order to carry out the teaching of the philosophical tradition.[1] The *guru-sisya* relationship remained a central institution of philosophical Hinduism and of religious Hinduism.

Gonda (1965:275-83) maintains that in the last millenium the Indian *guru,* though accommodating himself to changing circumstances, has essentially remained the same personage, with the same qualities and functions, even though he has not always been a brahmin or an ascetic, but might have been a man of any caste. Gonda accounts for the central place of the *guru* in terms of several factors. The *guru* is believed to be the bearer of sacred knowledge and tradition, to hold the secret of divine mysteries, and to be a person in peculiarly close communion with the Highest Being, whether on account of asceticism, utterances regarded as inspired, or saintliness of life or character. McMullen (1982:134) notes, moreover, that an absence of a unified and systematic religious doctrine and dogma and the lack of an ecclesiastical organization facilitated the development of the centrality of the concept of the *guru* who, with charismatic authority, interpreted the scriptures and pointed a way to liberation.

The Hindu scriptures distinguish between three kinds of *guru:* (1) the divine Guru; (2) the inner guru; and (3) the human guru (Prabuddha Bharata, 1979:282-7). The divine Guru is the only Guru, the ultimate Guru (*Gītā*, 9.18), and, according to various schools of philosophy, is referred to as Brahman, Saccidānanda, Sadguru, the Supreme Teacher, the Creator of all creators, the Word *(Vak)*, *Avatāra* (that is, incarnations of God as Teacher, such as Sri Krishna, Buddha, Christ, Sankara, Sri Ramakrishna and others). The inner guru is the awakened spiritual faculty of one's own mind (the "third eye" or "the inner eye" or the *sattvika buddhi* of Gitä 18.30), which guides the aspirant to God-realization. The human guru is the agent who awakens the inner guru and brings about the union of the individual spirit with the Supreme Spirit.

The human guru, as agent or instrument, has four main functions: (a) to instruct the disciple in the spiritual ideal and means of attaining it; (b) to awaken the power of spiritual intuition; (c) to remove egoism by correction; and (d) to connect the disciple to a particular spiritual tradition. The human guru is believed to embody the spirit of guidance. Ultimately this is to be found within oneself (the inner guru). Rāmana Mahārshi (1972:480) taught that God manifests himself as the human guru only to guide the devotee[2] to find the Self (the true Guru, God) within. For Rāmana Mahārshi (1972:*passim),* God, Guru and self are one. His philosophy is pure *advaita* (non-duality).

In the Hindu tradition, the human guru mediates his personal God-experience. The guru is regarded as the medium through whom God reveals himself to the disciple (Gonda, 1965:282); hence the peculiar veneration of the *guru* in the diversity of philosophies and sectarian forms of Hinduism. The *guru-sisya* relationship is conceived as a sacred bond based on the total involvement, commitment and obligation of two persons who are bound to each other forever. The *Dharmasutras* lay down in detail the relationship between the teacher and the taught, and also prescribe a rule of conduct in respect of the teacher. The disciple questions, listens, obeys, serves and worships the *guru*. The disciple treats the *guru* with reverence and with those symbolic rituals (such as touching the feet of the *guru*) which are usually directed toward God. The *guru* assumes responsibility for the spiritual growth of the disciple and acts as a channel for divine grace (Prabuddha Bharata, 1979:283).

Dikṣā (initiation) establishes formally the *guru-sisya* relationship. In the initiation ceremony, the *guru* is believed to transmit his divine power to the disciple. Initiation usually takes the form of communication of a *mantra* (sacred name or formula), but it may also be by touch, by sight or by thought. According to Rāmana Mahārshi (1972:370,444), *mauna* (silence) is the best and most potent *dikṣā*, the other methods (look, touch, word) being of a lower order and derived from silence. The *guru's* silence is the loudest *upadesa* (teaching) and grace in its highest form (Gonda, 1965:461-62). It is expected that initiation brings about the desired fruit in time (Acharuparambil, 1980:20-9). In contemporary twentieth-century Hindu society, a priest still initiates a young brahmin male into his class through the sacred thread ceremony and receives from the young man the homage due to the *guru* (Cole, 1982:3).

Osborne (1980:133) has noted a further point about the *guru-sisya* relationship; namely, the possibility of following a *guru* who is no longer physically embodied (e.g., Rāmana Mahārshi, Swāmi Rāmdās, Swāmi Sivānanda, Sri Ramakrishna). The disciples of these gurus who have left the body are in no less certainty as to their guidance than those who followed them in their lifetime.

I have noted in the introductory chapter the centrality of the guru-disciple relationship in the social construction of an ashram. There has been much discussion among Christian ashramites as to what makes an ashram "really an ashram" and as to what is the position of the guru in this regard. All Christian ashramites, leaders and followers, Protestant and Catholic, regard Christ as the true Guru who is central to the origin and the ongoing life of the ashram (Beaver,1965:887; Abhishiktānanda, 1970b:74,1313; 1974:202; Vandana, 1978b:51-2; Griffiths, 1982:24). The relationship between the three kinds of *guru* is of particular importance in the ideology of the Christian ashram movement. Abhishiktānanda (1970a:131-33; 1974:202) distinguishes between the instrumental *(karak)* guru, who leads the disciple to experiential knowledge of God, and the true Guru (the *Sadguru*), Christ. In the Christian ashram, the human guru witnesses not simply from his or her own experience, but from the experience of Christ, the

Sadguru, who alone introduces the disciple to the Real and reveals the Inner Guru (the Spirit) within the heart of the disciple (Abhishiktānanda, 1974:202). Vandana (1975a:130; 1984a:38) also makes the distinction between the instrumental *(karak)* guru who leads the disciple on to the True or Real Guru, Christ (the *Sadguru),* and to the Indweller or Spirit of Christ (the *Antaryamin).*

Protestants and Catholics differ, however, in their attitude, teaching, and ideology concerning the position and role of the human guru, and in their conception of the locus of authority. Catholic ashrams lay great stress on the centrality of the individual human guru, who exercises personal charismatic authority. Abhishiktānanda (1970b:74) states clearly that the real ashram is not so much in the huts where the ashramites live "as in the heart of a guru who lives there and in his personal contact in the depth with the Indweller." Vandana (1975b:352; 1978a:16; 1984a:38) takes the same position. So too does Dom Bede Griffiths (1982:24) when he describes an ashram as "a group of disciples gathered around a master, or guru, who come to share the prayer life, the experience of God, of the guru." Protestant ashramites tend to attach less importance to the role of a human guru (much as Gandhi refused to accept the role of guru). In the Protestant ashrams, Christ is perceived as the only Guru of a fellowship of Christian disciples. Hence, authority is seen to rest in the community as a whole, rather than in one person, and consensus is regarded as the ideal mode of decision-making. A founder may be regarded as a charismatic prophet who inspired the initiation of the community. Sometimes the human guru is perceived as central to the formation and maintenance of unity in the community (Beaver, 1965:887).

In the ideology of the Christian ashram movement (as well as in the Hindu tradition), the charismatic guru is generally regarded as the central religious personality from whose personal religious experience and inspiration the ashram is created and upon whose authority the guru-disciple relationship is based (Vandana, 1978b:51-2; Griffiths, 1982:24). The guru-disciple relationship is considered a necessary condition for the creation of the community. In a Christian ashram, therefore, the relationship of the members with one another as members of the Body of Christ through the Eucharist (in the Catholic tradition), or as a Christian Fellowship (in the Protestant tradition) constructs and sustains the life of the ashram community. Ashram literature and ideology, particularly in the Catholic ashram movement, tend to neglect the fact that the *sufficient* condition for the creation and continuing existence of the community is the ongoing *relationship* between guru and disciples.

4. *Sādhanā*. The Sanskrit terms for the ways or paths to salvation are *sādhanā*, *mārga* and *yoga*. The term *sādhanā* refers to the "means or method of effecting or achieving a particular end" (Stutley, 1977:277); it is "the course of spiritual discipline or teaching, leading to the fulfilment or realization of life" (Parrinder, 1971:239-40). It involves strenuous spiritual effort and various ascetic mental and devotional disciplines, much as the stages of life in *āsrama dharma* demand specific duties which are to be carried out in an attitude of spiritual obligation. Swāmi Sivānanda (n.d.:47) exhorts his disciples to "carefully observe the five 'do-nots'" during the period of *sādhanā;* that is, not to mix much, because mixing will cause disturbance of the mind; not to talk much, because talking will cause distractions; not to walk much, because walking will cause exhaustion and weakness; not to eat much, because eating much induces laziness and sleep; not to sleep much. In other words, *sādhanā* implies disciplined moderation in all things.

Every *sādhanā* is chosen to meet the particular needs of a person and to achieve spiritual progress. The *guru* initiates the disciple into a particular *sādhanā*. All *sādhanās* are methods for the imperfect disciple to attain *moksa* (liberation; that is, release from time and space and from the continuous cycle of birth, death and rebirth). The goal of every *sādhanā* is to return to Ultimate Reality, whether conceived as impersonal Absolute Brahman or as a personal God. The disciple aspires to God-realization, which for the non-dualist *advaitins* is conceived as merging into identity with Brahman; and for the followers of theistic sects and cults, as union with a personal God (Dhavamony, 1966:78).

All religious traditions have specific *sādhanās* for their followers. The *sādhaka* is one who feels prompted to follow a particular *sādhanā*. The spiritual guides of the Christian tradition, as well as the *gurus* and *ācāryas* of the Indian tradition, formulate for their disciples common or personal *sādhanās*. Such are the various monastic orders of the Hindu and Christian tradition. So too the *gurus* and charismatic personalities around whom an ashram, whether Hindu or Christian, is formed, prescribe common and personal *sādhanās* for their followers. The specific *sādhanā* of an ashram is a major factor contributing to the unique character of the ashram. The spiritual discipline of the ashram is regarded as providing the motive force and dynamism for action (Beaver, 1965:887).

5. *Mārga. Mārga* means the way or path to *moksa* (liberation). There are three principal *mārgas:* (1) *karma-mārga,* involving work, the performance of ascetical and religious observance; (2) *bhakti-mārga,* involving loving devotion and surrender to a personal God; and (3) *jñāna-mārga,* involving transcendental knowledge of Reality (Parrinder, 1971:177). In actual practice, no *mārga* is followed in isolation, each being combined with elements of another; nevertheless, the three *mārgas* can be distinguished analytically (Dhavamony, 1966:78; 1982:468). In the Hindu tradition, the three *mārgas* are identified with the three forms of *yoga: karma-yoga, bhakti-yoga* and *jñāna-yoga*; particularly as they are outlined in the *Yoga Sutras* by Patañjali, the philosopher of the second century B.C. Various schools of philosophy have developed other *mārgas,* many of them involving one or other form of yoga. All of them underline the importance of the *guru* to initiate and guide the aspirant or disciple in the path of self-realization.

Conclusion

The analytical distinctions which are made between the *mārgas* cast light on the empirical expression and the meaning of different kinds of ashrams. In the Hindu tradition, the three *mārgas* are the basis for the construction of specific types of ashrams. As the *guru* teaches a particular path to salvation, the disciples who listen to his or her message gather around and become a following. The message is the dynamic element of a community which is characteristically a *karma*-type, a *bhakti*-type or a *jñāna*-type ashram community. Thus one can identify the Gandhian ashrams, *Satyāgraha* and *Sevāgrām,* as realizations of the *karma-mārga* type; *Anandashram,* founded by Swāmi Rāmdās, and characterized by much chanting, singing and joy, as a *bhakti-mārga* type; and *Rāmanāshramam,* which developed around Rāmana Mahārshi, as closely realizing a *jñāna-mārga* type ashram. The actual ashram never exhibits a pure-type, but rather a mixture of all three *mārgas* being followed, with one or another dominating. In Chapter 6, I will examine in greater detail some contemporary Hindu ashrams to show how they exemplify the different *mārgas*.

Christian ashrams can be described and analyzed in a similar manner. Broadly speaking, two distinct types of Christian ashrams have developed: (1) the evangelical Protestant social service and social action-oriented ashrams; and (2) the Catholic contemplative and monastic-oriented ashrams. The former were the first to appear historically in the first half of this century;[3] the latter appeared after independence. The evangelical Protestant ashrams, which emphasize social action and social service for the promotion of the Kingdom of God, most closely fit the *karma-mārga* type; on the other hand, the Orthodox Syrian and Roman Catholic ashrams, while recognizing the validity of, and sometimes illustrating, *karma-mārga,* tend more commonly to emphasize *jñāna-mārga* or *bhakti-mārga*. I describe these different types of Christian ashrams in Chapters 7 and 8, respectively.

Notes

[1]The five *ācāryas* were Sankara (788-820 A.D.), Ramanuja (ca. 1017 A.D.), Nimbarka (ca. 1162 A.D.), Madhva (1199-1278) and Vallabha (ca. 1500 A.D.).

[2]Rāmana Mahārshi claimed no disciples; hence he always used the term devotee, rather than disciple.

[3]*Christukula* ashram, a Protestant ashram which was founded in 1921 by Savarirayan Jesudason and E. Forrester Paton, is usually identified as the first Christian ashram. My field work revealed, however, that an Orthodox Syrian ashram, *Bethany* ashram, which was founded in 1918 in Ranni-Perunad in Central Travancore (now Kerala) by Father P. T. Geevarghese (later to become Archbishop Mar Ivanios, who left the ashram to found the Syro-Malankara rite, an affiliate of the Roman Catholic Church). Father P. T. Geevarghese was on the staff of Serampore College, West Bengal, from 1913 to 1918. There he prepared a group of young Orthodox Syrian Christian seminarians for a monastic life which drew from the traditions and life-style of early Christian monasticism, from his contacts with the Anglican Oxford Mission in Calcutta, as well as from the revived ashram tradition of Hinduism (Gibbons, 1962:19-27). *Bethany* ashram exists today as a monastic community which still aims to integrate some aspects of traditional Indian culture with Orthodox Syrian monasticism. I will describe it in Chapter 8.

CHAPTER 6

CONTEMPORARY HINDU ASHRAMS:
THE THREE WAYS

As I have observed in Chapter 3, the revival of the ancient ashram tradition was a significant aspect of the reform movements of late nineteenth and early twentieth century Hinduism. The religious leaders of these movements communicated a message which embodied one or more of the dominant *mārgas* as the appropriate way to follow toward *moksa*. Insofar as followers heeded the message and responded., ashrams developed a characteristic structure, ideology and project of life.

The Ramakrishna Order (Math and Mission)

Among the ashram revival movements, the Ramakrishna movement is one of the best known, particularly in the West, and the most enduring.[1] Sri Ramakrishna was a poor Bengali brahmin priest at the Dakshineswar temple of the Divine Mother in the form of Kali, outside Calcutta. His extraordinary spiritual gifts drew many followers among village and urban dwellers, the educated and the illiterate. His teachings appealed particularly to young English-educated Bengalis who were caught up in the Neo-Hindu reform movements. They also had an important influence on changing the image of woman in Indian society (King, 1984:73-4). Ramakrishna worshipped the Divine Mother in the form of his wife, Sarada Devi, who became his first disciple and who received initiation from him. After Ramakrishna's death in 1886, Sarada Devi became a guru in her own right.

By 1880 a small Ramakrishna movement had formed. Outstanding among the disciples was Narendranath Datta, the future Swāmi Vivekānanda, who was designated by Ramakrishna as his spiritual heir. Vivekānanda was a charismatic (and controversial) leader in his own right. Whereas Ramakrishna was par excellence a *bhaktāyogi*, a spiritual leader who emphasized devotion, who regarded all religions as true, and who led his disciples to God-realization through their own religion; Vivekānanda was a *karmayogi,* who led the movement to work in the world through education, medical service, social welfare, uplift of the masses, and relief in times of calamity.

In its origins, the Ramakrishna movement was founded on the personal relationship between Sri Ramakrishna and his disciples. In the early stages after the death of the founder, the direction in which the movement was to develop became problematic. Ramakrishna's disciples refused to accept the legitimacy of Vivekānanda's proposals for a radical commitment to social reform and his criticism of excessive devotionalism. Vivekānanda became a wandering and missionary *sannyāsi*. On the basis of his personal charisma, he gathered his own disciples; in India, attracting those seeking reform and modernity; in America and Britain, appealing to those seeking Eastern philosophy and spirituality. On his return to India from abroad, he founded, in 1897, the Ramakrishna Order (Math and Mission).

Like Ramakrishna, Vivekānanda also promoted the status of women. He believed that *sannyāsinis* could contribute to national development. He was concerned about giving women access to modern scientific education as well as religious education, and not confining them to work in the home (King, 1984:75-6). Nevertheless, the Ramakrishna Order was a strictly male institution. Although Sarada Devi was the symbolic religious head of the Order until her death in 1920, the real head was the male President of the Order. It was not until 1954, after Indian independence, that a separate and organizationally independent women's branch of the Ramakrishna Order, the Sri Sarada Math and Ramakrishna Sarada Mission, was founded.

Vivekānanda was clearly influenced by Christian and Western organizational structures and patterns. He integrated the Hindu traditions of *sannyāsa* (renunciation) and of *karma* (selfless service) with Christian models of monastic and apostolic orders, to create a new religious movement. As the movement spread throughout India and beyond to Europe and North America, it rapidly became institutionalized into a complex, bureaucratic organization with a routinized spirituality, a routinized order of monks, a routinized mission, and a routinized authority. In the contemporary Ramakrishna Order, *maths* and ashrams are considered to be synonymous. Ramakrishna *maths*, and convents established for women, tend to be like monasteries, where authority has become rationalized. Every ashram has a guru, who can initiate members, but commitment and obedience of the members are to the organization rather than to the individual guru. The President of the Ramakrishna Order is the one supreme guru of the organization. He is regarded as the personification of Sri Ramakrishna and is responsible to give the *mantra* (sacred name or prayer formula) to each member. Within the structure of the organization, charisma has become rationalized to locate authority and administrative leadership in the Swāmis of the Order. In its *maths* and missions, the Order has combined the two ways of *jñāna-mārga* and *karma-mārga*.

Sri Rāmanāshramam

In contrast to both Sri Ramakrishna and Swāmi Vivekānanda, Rāmana Mahārshi (1879-1950) was a brahmin-born Tamil mystic and *jñānayogi* who led the life of an ascetic on the sacred mountain of Arunāchala.[2] Although he wrote and said little, his powerful presence and message attracted many disciples. Thousands came, often merely to be in his presence, because in the Hindu tradition the sight of a holy person *(darshana)* has spiritual merit. Among them were Monchanin and Le Saux, the founders of the first Catholic ashram.[3] According to Rāmana Mahārshi (1972:370,444), silence is the best and the most powerful form of initiation of the disciple. The guru's silence is considered to be the loudest teaching and grace in its highest form (Gonda, 1965:461-2). He taught that God manifests himself as the human guru only to guide the devotee to find the Self (the true Guru, God) within. For Rāmana Mahārshi (1972:*passim*), God, Guru, and self are one. His philosophy was pure Vedāntic non-duality *(advaita)*. His message was to follow the Vedāntic path of self-knowledge.

Rāmana Mahārshi never concerned himself with social action or reform movements. Nevertheless, he acknowledged the spiritual power *(adhyatma shakti)* working in Gandhi and leading him on. He advised others to cultivate similar disinterestedness and self-surrender to a higher power. He taught that work *(karma yoga)* can well go hand in hand with worship *(bhakti yoga)*; that devotion leads to self-surrender and it may be "to any idea, to any form of God, to a *satguru*, to humanity in general, to the idea of beauty or justice."[4] Various writings of Rāmana Mahārshi indicate that, although he was clearly a *jñānayogi*, like Gandhi, Vivekānanda and Aurobindo, he valued social service, international brotherhood and equality as the mark and measure of moral excellence and spiritual realization. His followers created the ashram community which, after his death, became the basis of a large contemporary organization, *Sri Rāmanāshramam,* centred on the guru's institutionalized message and administered by a Board of Trustees. Rāmana Mahārshi's message has become routinized and rationalized in the publications of *Rāmanāshramam*; in particular, collections of the guru's words of guidance during his lifetime and a quarterly publication, "The Mountain Path." About seventy men (no women) are permanent residents, while hundreds of visitors, men and women, foreign and Indian, visit the ashram for varying periods.   A manager is the administrative head of the ashram.   The reality of the ashram, however, is structured around the power of the presence of the now dead guru and his relationship with his devotees. There is no community life among the ashramites. Some devotees or disciples of Rāmana Mahārshi are guided by individual Swāmis of the ashram. The ashram is recognized among Hindus and Christians as an authentic source of the Vedāntic path of self-knowledge.

Sri Gñānānanda Memorial Trust (Thapovanam Ashram)

Not far from *Rāmanāshramam,* near Tyrukkoyilur in Tamil Nadu, is Thapovanam, the ashram which was created and constructed by disciples who gathered around the person of Swāmi Gñānānanda some thirty years ago. The ashram was formed for those who listened to his message and wished to devote time to the pursuit of wisdom and follow the path of *jñāna yoga.* Swāmi Gñānānanda was a mysterious personage; he never spoke of his birth or his parentage and he lived for more than a century, his death occurring in 1974. His philosophy, spiritual teachings and way of life had a great influence on Henri Le Saux, in the early days of *Shāntivanam* (Abhishiktānanda, 1970a). He taught that silent meditation *(dhyāna)* is the only thing necessary for liberation, but he recognized that *pūjā* (ceremonies), *japa* (repetition of the *mantra*), devotions, rites and the rest are useful, especially for beginners. Hence he built a small temple with deities, and his discourses abound with references to the importance of worship of the personal God with form. *Sannyāsins,* who practise silent meditation, live alongside *bhaktās,* who spend their time singing *bhajans* (chants) and *kirtans* (songs of praise which often tell a story). The ashram attempts to preserve the ancient Vedic culture; Vedic chants are sung during the *pūjās.* An important place is also given to Tamil devotional and mystic lore.

The organization of Thapovanam presents a pattern not met with in orthodox Hindu ashrams. In Sri Gñānānanda's thinking, the interaction of people in all stages of life is mutually beneficial. Hence, one finds *sannyāsins* and *brahmachārins* living side by side with retired householders, as well as others who work. The families of householders, women and children, participate in the daily worship and life of the ashram. The *guru's* presence, in his *samādhi* (the last stage of yogic concentration; also death; represented by his sacred tomb), is still the focal point of the ashram. There is no "successor" to Sri Gñānānanda; rather, Swāmi Nityānanda Giri holds the position of *āchārya.*[5] At Thapovanam, the Hindu monastic revival is nurtured; at the same time, seekers and disciples of Sri Gñānānanda may stay for varying periods of time to perform their individual *sādhanās* in a suitable environment, where they are in contact with Sadguru Gñānānanda's grace (the *guru prasād)*. In the hills near Salem, at Yircand, in 1969, Sri Gñānānanda formed a centre where monks and disciples devote themselves solely to the silent meditation and study of *jñāna-mārga*; there are no rituals or common worship at this centre.

Sāntiniketan Ashram and Sri Aurobindo Ashram

Two other important Hindu ashrams of the early twentieth century persist today, albeit in changed form: *Sāntiniketan* ashram and *Aurobindo* ashram. Rabindranath Tagore, India's greatest modern poet and prolific writer of diverse literary genres, developed *Sāntiniketan* ashram in 1901 from the 1863 ashram of his father, Devendranath Tagore.[6] There he established a *gurukula*, in the classic Hindu tradition of instructing the disciple or religious student in the guru's house. Students shared the life of the master, caste lines were broken, and the community developed a life-style integrated with nature, which exemplified both *jñāna-mārga* and *bhakti-mārga*.

Rabindrananth Tagore was a philosopher, musician and artist, as well as poet and educationist. A Brahmo Samajist, who was both product and producer of a syncretized modern Bengali and Western consciousness and culture, Rabindranath Tagore (Gurudev, as he was called) was without question a charismatic guru for those who accepted his mystic view of life. While Tagore was alive, the ashram life-style and authority structure rested on his charismatic power. His idealistic and revolutionary educational structure became a centre of international learning and culture and was transformed into Visva-Bhārati University of today. A minority of followers continue the semblance of an ashram life structure in the context of the highly rationalized Visva-Bhārati University, with its several departments and the concomitant problems of bureaucratic conflict over organizational goals, structure, process and power.

Sri Aurobindo ashram is a flourishing contemporary Hindu ashram.[7] Most important among the disciples who gathered around Sri Arobindo in the colony of Pondicherry was a French woman, Mira Richard, who came to stay with him from 1920 until his death. Known as "the Mother," she was in charge of *Sri Aurobindo* ashram from its official foundation in 1926 until her own death in 1973. Sri

Aurobindo's charismatic authority was transferred to her; in a meticulously organized large ashram she commanded unquestioned obedience. Visitors to the ashram today are struck by the sense of peace, and, even more, by the discipline of the ashram life and activities. According to ashram ideology, the outer work and discipline signify the inner spirit of discipline and integration. It is thus a conscious attempt to integrate *jñāna-mārga* and *karma-mārga*. The ashram members today number more than two thousand, among them many Westerners; they live in various dwellings among the four hundred buildings owned by the ashram throughout Pondicherry. The ashram is self-sufficient in food, clothing and shelter. Some twenty-eight departments are administered by a five-member Board of Trustees. Although the ideology stresses freedom and a conception of work as unpaid service among equals, at least some ashramites and visitors define the reality of ashram life as rigidly controlled. "The Mother," even more than Sri Aurobindo, remains a dominant symbolic guru of the ashram.

Kanyā Kumāri Sthān

The transference of charismatic authority from a founding guru to a principal woman disciple, who has, in turn, become a guru for her disciples, is illustrated in two other ashrams. One is *Kanyā Kumāri Sthān*, Sakori, Maharashtra, which was founded by Sri Upāsani Baba (who was a disciple of Sai Baba of Shirdi) in 1917. This is a *bhakti-mārga* women's ashram, now led by Godāvari Mātāji, who was initiated into *sannyāsa* by Upāsani Baba and became leader of the ashram upon his death in 1941.[8]

The women are unmarried; they are believed to be the spouses of Krishna. The term *kanyā* refers to closeness to God; hence she is a woman who can lead one to God. The women wear colourful saris (not the customary ochre-coloured *kavi* of *sannyāsinis*), gold bangles and jewelry. They have traditional brahmin men's roles, such as chanting the Vedas and performing the Vedic sacrifice. The sensory effect of the ashram, with its bright colours, joyful songs, dancing and relaxation, is in sharp contrast to the austere renunciation of other ashrams. Upāsani Baba's *bhakti* way of devotional service of Krishna and his teachings have become routinized in a rationally organized institution. At the same time, Godāvari Mātāji's charismatic authority is the legitimated source of the ashram's ongoing reality.

Ānandashram

A second *bhakti-mārga* ashram now under the leadership of a principal woman disciple of the founder is *Ānandashram*, Kanhangad, Kerala. It was founded in 1931 by Swāmi Rāmdās (1884-1963), known to his followers as "Beloved Bapa," who was in his turn a disciple of Sri Rāmana Mahārshi. Krishnabai Mātāji (1903-), a widow who joined him as a permanent disciple in 1928, became his spiritual successor. Although over eighty years old and an invalid, her personal charisma is recognized by a large following of ashramites and visiting devotees. Since the death of Swāmi Rāmdās, she continues to be the focal point of the ashram, with the ashram's one *sannyāsi* exercising a managerial role.[9] She, in her turn, identifies Swāmi Rāmdās as the only guru. For her, God, her guru (Swāmi Rāmdās) and herself are indeed one. She follows exclusively the *bhakti* way of repetition of the Divine Name *(Rām Nām)* to attain God-realization.[10] The characteristic feature of the ashram is the continuous chanting, by individuals or groups, of *Rām Nām*, the *mantra-japa* of Swāmi Rāmdās. The buildings of the ashram have been constructed by devotees, who tend to be regular annual visitors; the permanent ashram members are few.

Brahma Vidyā Mandir

Brahma Vidyā Mandir ashram near Wardha, Maharashtra, the contemporary ashram of women disciples of Vinoba Bhave's *boodhan* movement, is organized somewhat differently from either *Kanyā Kumāri* ashram or *Ānandashram*. The name of the ashram means 'House of the Knowledge of God.' The ashram was founded by Vinoba Bhave in 1959, according to the principles and life-style of Gandhiji's *Sevāgrām* ashram, where Vinoba Bhave had been in charge. It was established with twelve young women who had participated for varying periods of time (some of them for ten to twelve years) in the movement's land reform march throughout India between 1951 and the mid-seventies. Initially, Vinoba Bhave did not live with the community, but he was always the guru who guided it; he lived there in his retirement. Today, Vinoba Bhave, although disembodied, remains the charismatic guru of the members of the ashram.[11]

The ashram members follow a path of *karma mārga*, which means every kind of work necessary to attain 'Knowledge of God' (in conformity with the ashram name). Their spirituality is based on *Advaita* (non-duality) philosophy and the *Bhagavad Gītā*. They follow a simple life-style which includes silence, meditation and a collective striving for knowledge of God, and which seeks unification of science and religion, according to Vinoba Bhave's teachings. In keeping with these teachings, they regularly chant the Vedas (usually the prerogative of a twice-born Hindu male); they sometimes spin while they meditate; each day they spend several hours in productive work, whether it be publishing, or manual labour in the ashram fields or household. Authority is exercised through collective decision-making and reference to the teachings and writings of Vinoba.

Sivānandāshram (Divine Life Society)

Perhaps the most influential Hindu ashram for the Catholic ashram movement has been *Sivānandāshram*, Rishikesh. Swāmi Sivānanda (1887-1963), a Tamil and a medical doctor by profession, worked in Malaya until his spiritual conversion in 1923. He returned home to devote his life to God-realization. He attracted disciples who formed a community around him on the banks of the sacred Ganges, near Rishikesh in the foothills of the Himalayas. In 1934, he settled with four disciples in a small kutir, *Ananda Kutir*, which was to be his home until his death in 1963. Land nearby was acquired for the the construction of *Sivānandāshram*. From the ashram emerged the Divine Life Society, a large contemporary organization, which was legally registered in 1936 as a religious trust society, which is administered by five constitutionally defined bodies, and which has branches all over the world. Its headquarters are *Sivānandāshram*, near Rishikesh.[12]

Swāmi Sivānanda taught the Vedānta and several forms of yoga; he wrote prolifically--about yogic systems, about Hindu philosophy and religion, about *ayurvedic* medicine--and he produced a translation and commentary on the *Bhagavadgītā*. He also empasized various types of social service, particularly medical service. This ashram demonstrates the routinization of charisma in a rational organization which has institutionalized the teachings, writings and actions of the founder. As well as housing the permanent *sannyāsis, brahmachāris, sādhakas* and servants, the ashram has countless devotees, pilgrims, long- and short-term visitors and guests, so that the residents may number several hundred, even in the winter months. Swāmi Sivānanda attracted many highly educated and talented men and women as his disciples. Several of them have become outstanding charismatic gurus in their own right and have extended the Divine Life Society, not only throughout the Indian sub-continent, but also to North America, Europe and Australia.

The elected President of the Divine Life Society, Swāmi Chidānanda, presents himself to the ashram members and to the outside world as a disciple of the founding guru, Swāmi Sivānanda. In his own right, Swāmi Chidānanda exercises charismatic spiritual leadership, while the day-to-day running of the ashram, its departments, and its branches is rationally organized under the authority of the Secretary-General of the Divine Life Society, Swāmi Krishnānanda, a brilliant philosopher and scholar. Senior *swāmis* or *sannyāsis* are in charge of various departments, such as the library, the kitchen and dining-hall, the printing, the *bhajan* hall and the yoga classes.

Swāmi Sivānanda believed that *karma-yoga* and the Vedānta are integral and complementary to each other (Gyan, 1980:71). He also affirmed *bhakti-yoga* as a valid way to salvation by conducting *kirtans* and *bhajan*-chanting throughout the country. The disciples and devotees who flock to *Sivānandāshram*, especially during the summer months, follow the founding guru's message in any or all of the three *mārgas,* depending on who is their individual guru. They will participate in all, or some, or even none of the ashram's daily yoga classes, *pūjās, bhajan*-chanting, and *satsang*. Some will be students in the ashram's Yoga-Vedanta Forest Academy. Westerners, as well as Indians, may become relatively long-term visitors who remain for months or even years; these persons will have a clearly-defined *sādhanā* prescribed by their individual gurus.

Sivānandāshram (Bihar School of Yoga)

An important disciple of Swāmi Sivānanda, Guru Swāmi Satyānanda Saraswati (1923-), became the founder of another ashram, which is wholly dedicated to *karma yoga*. Swāmi Satyānanda was a follower of Swāmi Sivānanda in the early days of the Rishikesh ashram, received *sannyāsa* in 1943, and was initiated into the monastic order of Saraswati by Swāmi Sivānanda in 1947. According to Hindu monastic tradition, he was a wandering *sannyāsi* for nine years, during which time he perfected his own *sādhanā*. He established an ashram, originally named *Sivānandāshram,* on the banks of the Ganges, at Monghyr in eastern Bihar.[13] In 1962 he founded the International Yoga Fellowship; in 1964 the ashram became known as the Bihar School of Yoga. In twenty years, the original ashram has developed eighty ashrams and six hundred affiliated centres in practically every country in the world.

In its early days, the ashram was a place to train swāmis, to help people through yoga, and to start yoga centres. People would come for courses of a week, two weeks, a month or longer. Swāmi Satyānanda would initiate some into *sannyāsa diksha,* after a probationary period of no fixed duration. The ashram teaches no particular form of religion or philosophy. It is conceived as being a community moved by one spirit, one common goal; the members retain their social identity, yet work toward spiritual development through *karma yoga.* The membership now numbers about five thousand swāmis, approximately twenty percent of these being in twenty-five ashrams in Australia. At the ashram in Bihar, there are about seventy to eighty swāmis in residence, some sixty per cent of these being foreign. The striking features of the membership are the dominance of foreigners (men and women), their youth, and the responsible tasks they perform in the running of the ashram and its affiliates. Guru Swāmi Satyānanda has now named an Australian, Swāmi Niranjin, as President of the Bihar School of Yoga; he is responsible for the ashram life and activities. Nevertheless, Guru Swāmi Satyānanda Saraswati clearly remains the only guru of the ashram and its symbolic head. Great preparations were under way to receive him with high honour and reverence soon after my visit.

The main activities of the ashram are teaching and training in all forms of yoga, publishing, and now, above all, research into yoga. Yoga courses are offered in schools, factories and prisons, as well as at the ashram. Courses at the ashram tend to be offered for foreigners in the cooler months between November and February, and for Indians between March and October. At the time of my visit, a very large, modern, Western-style, multi-storey building was under construction to provide more appropriate facilities for all these activities. Among the membership are trained scientists, medical doctors, and psychiatrists, who are eminently equipped to carry on research into yoga. The daily routine of the ashram is a life of *karma mārga*. The young members rise at five and are kept very busy all day--in gardening, in cultivating and preparing food, in publishing and printing, in accounting, in teaching, learning or research in various forms of yoga.

In typical monastic style, silence is the practice during work; the teaching is that one meditates while one engages in *karma yoga*. There is early morning prayer, and in the evening a half-hour of joyful *kirtans* (songs that tell a story). The *gurukul* (in the traditional Hindu style of teachers and students living and learning together) trains the youth of the ashram. These are treated as adults; noone rebukes them and they are given total freedom to develop self-responsibility. All the members wear the ochre-coloured *kavi* robe and have shaven heads, which characterize *sannyāsa*.

Omkarānanda Ashram

Omkarānanda ashram is named for its founder and guru, Swāmi Omkarānanda, who also became a disciple of Swāmi Sivānanda. At the age of seventeen years he joined Swāmi Sivānanda, was later initiated into *sannyāsa,* and then sent by him to found an ashram near Zurich, Switzerland. The ashram has become a large community of families. In 1983, an ashram in Rishikesh, quite close to *Sivānandāshram,* was founded.[14] Here a small group of six or seven Indians, together with two Swiss *sannyāsinis* (who grew up from childhood in the Swiss ashram), are heavily engaged in *karma yoga* in the construction of the ashram and its grounds. The most striking feature of the ashram is that twice a week the ashramite women make *havan.* According to the Hindu woman who accompanied and instructed me, they conduct the ritual and chant the Vedic *mantras* impeccably.

Conclusion

The evidence of my research clearly indicates that in the Hindu ashram tradition, charismatic authority has remained significant. Each ashram has been constructed around the relationship between guru and disciples. The guru proclaims a message, by silence, word or example, which points a way for the disciples to follow: *jñāna-mārga, bhakti-mārga*, or *karma-mārga*, or some combination of these. Charisma has become routinized during the lifetime of the guru, and an institutionalized community has developed. Rational patterns of authority have emerged, with the guru exercising spiritual authority. Sometimes he or she remains actively involved in day-to-day decision-making; sometimes he or she withdraws entirely from mundane affairs. When the guru is no longer in the body (or voluntarily withdraws from active leadership), the structure of authority varies. At times a designated leading disciple continues to exercise charismatic authority; at other times, a clearly defined rational structure is established, particularly when the ashram wishes to register as a religious trust under state laws. Always the founding guru retains symbolic spiritual authority and serves as the *raison d'être* of the ashram. If the message continues to appeal, then the ashram will continue to flourish; if it no longer rings true, then the ashram will decline or die.

Notes

[1] My information about the Ramakrishna movement comes from a talk given by Swāmi Chidānanda, Acting President of Ramakrishna Mission, Bangalore, 21 October, 1983, and an interview with Swāmi Lokeswarānanda, Secretary, Ramakrishna Mission Institute of Culture, Gol Park, Calcutta, 21 March, 1984. Useful references are Williams (1981) and Singh (1983).

[2] I visited Sri Rāmanāshramam, 27-29 February, 1984, and interviewed the manager, Sri T. Sriniwasan, as well as visitors to the ashram. Like the devotees, I made a four-hour ritualistic *giri-pradakshina*, that is, a clockwise circuit around the sacred mountain, keeping the mountain to my right side, as is the custom when one circumambulates any holy place or object. I also climbed the mountain and visited caves and *Skandashram*, where Rāmana Mahārshi lived for seven years. From the mountain, one has a spectacular view of the immense and beautiful Dravidian temple of Annāmalaiyār, where Sri Rāmana Mahārshi first dwelt at the foot of the mountain, in the town of Tiruvannāmalai. Abhishiktānanda (1979a) records the sacred story of the mountain of Arunāchala and of Sri Rāmana Mahārshi's association with it; for his fullest account of Sri Rāmana Mahārshi, see his book *Saccidānanda: A Christian Approach to Advaitic Experience* (Abhishiktānanda, 1974:19-40).

[3]See Chapter 4, above.

[4]From talks of Rāmana Mahārshi in Swāminathan (1979:121).

[5]I met Swāmi Nityānanda Giri when he was a guest at the Catholic Ashram Aikiya Satsang III, Bangalore, 18 to 22 October, 1983. There he discussed Sri Gñānānanda and described the ashram. He invited me to attend *Mahā Sivārate,* one of the greatest annual Hindu festivals, which fell on 29 February, 1984. He proved to be an invaluable and skilful teacher of the meaning of the various rituals, as well as an inspiring and gracious host.

[6]I visited *Sāntiniketan,* 27-30 March, 1984, and interviewed several ashramites and members of the university faculty, including Professor Ram Gandhi, grandson of Mahātma Gandhi. Ashram literature, especially an article written by Tagore in 1916 and reproduced in the Sāntiniketan golden jubilee publication of Visva-Bhārati (1951), provided additional reference material.

[7]I visited *Sri Aurobindo* ashram, 1-3 March, 1984, and interviewed the Senior Member of the Board of Trustees, the Head of Reception, a leading philosopher-guru (M. P. Pandit), and other members of the ashram.

[8]I visited *Kanyā Kumāri Sthān* ashram, 1-2 February, 1984, and interviewed Godāvari Mātāji (through an interpreter) and other ashram members. Useful references about the ashram and its history are Sahukar (1968) and Rao (1972).

[9]I visited *Anandashram,* 12-14 March, 1984, and interviewed Krishnabai Mātāji, the manager (Swāmi Satchidānanda), a linguist professor and disciple who cares for Krishnabai's personal needs at night, and other devotees of the ashram.

[10]Her autobiography (Krishnabai, 1964) is entitled *Guru's Grace* and is published by the ashram. When I asked Krishnabai to sign her autobiography, she wrote the *mantra-japa* which is continuously chanted in the ashram: *Om, Sri Rām, Jai Rām, Jai Jai Rām, Om.*

[11]As I have noted already in Chapter 3, I visited *Brahma Vidyā Mandir* ashram for an International Women's Conference, 8-12 November, 1983. Prior to that, 20 October, 1983, in Bangalore, I heard talks given by two elder sisters of the ashram, Ushabehn and Kusumbehn, about Vinoba Bhave's conception of the ashram and its present life-style. These women had walked with Vinobaji for as long as twelve years in his *bhoodan* march throughout India. See also Irudayaraj (1969) and Bahin (1970).

[12]I lived at *Sivānandāshram* for a month from 26 December, 1983, to 24 January, 1984, having previously paid several visits to the ashram. I had formal interviews with several leading swāmis and participated completely in the life of the ashram.

Each morning I was present for Swāmi Krishnānanda's daily *darshan*. Ananthanarayana (1970) has written Sivānanda's biography. Gyan (1980) and Miller (1981) have published studies of the ashram.

[13]I learned of Guru Swāmi Satyānanda and the Bihar School of Yoga from an Australian woman, Swāmi Alakhmurti, who visited *Sivānandāshram*, Rishikesh, in January 1984, and who invited me to visit Monghyr, which I did on April 3-4, 1984. Swāmi Alakhmurti was assigned to take care of me, and to arrange interviews with the President, Swāmi Niranjin, and other members of the ashram. I also visited three Australian ashrams between July and September, 1984.

[14]I visited *Omkarānanda* ashram on 19 January, 1984, and participated in the *havan* ritual the following morning, 20 January, 1984. Swāmi Vishvarupa chanted the Vedic *mantras*. My Hindu companion and instructor was Devi Menon.

CHAPTER 7

CONTEMPORARY CHRISTIAN ASHRAMS:

THE WAY OF ACTION

The evangelical Protestant ashrams are all characteristically dedicated to the way of selfless action and social service, whether or not there is explicit reference to the traditional Hindu teaching and practice of *karma mārga*. They are based on the Gandhian principles and message that ashrams are not only places for spiritual striving; they must also be oriented to social reconstruction.

Christukula Ashram

Christukula ashram,[1] the first Protestant ashram, is inter-denominational in character. As I have noted in Chapter 4, it was established by two medical missionaries, one an Indian, Dr. Savarirayan Jesudason, the other a Scot, Dr. Ernest Forrester Paton (Thomas, 1971:36). Both were concerned with the adoption of indigenous modes of evangelism and with the provision of medical and other social services (Savarirayan, 1981:7-9). Although the founders affiliated their work with the National Missionary Society, nevertheless, they believed that an essential feature of the ashram had to be autonomy; hence the ashram was established independent of control by ecclesiastical bodies or by foreign or national societies (Jesudason, 1939:576). Its management is vested by constitution in the *sevaks,* the servants of Christ, who are the permanent members of the ashram, and who control every aspect of ashram life and activity.

Jesudason (1937:2-7) consciously drew on the Vedic tradition in his conception of an ashram as a community of disciples gathered around a *guru,* who would train them in a *sādhanā* that would lead to the realization of a spiritual ideal. *Yoga,* particularly *karma yoga,* was proposed as the discipline for spiritual attainment (Rao, 1983:66). For Jesudason, as for other Christians, Christ is the *guru* of a Christian ashram; hence the name, *Christukula,* which means Christ's family. The constitution of the ashram allows for the election of one of the members as both spiritual and executive leader, or the division of these functions between two members. Perhaps these functions were divided during the lifetime of the founders, but since their death some fifteen to twenty years ago there has been one *āchārya* of the ashram, Dr. Raja Savarirayan, a nephew of the Indian founder, who has been a permanent member of the ashram since 1937. He attributes his conversion to the ashram way of life directly to his association and experience with Gandhi, who visited the ashram in 1935. By virtue of his association with the founders, Dr. Savarirayan exercises some charismatic authority as spiritual leader of the ashram. A medical doctor, he is also administrative head of the ashram hospital, dispensaries and eye clinics. The other three permanent members are in charge of specific aspects of ashram life and activities: maintaining the eighty-acre property and a dairy, a programme of non-formal education, direct evangelization, and extension work. It is expected, however, that decisions will ordinarily be consensual and unanimous.

The ashram is for men only; celibacy and renunciation of personal property are integral requirements of membership. The way to salvation as Christ's servants is presented and lived as *karma yoga,* selfless service. Jesudason (1939:583) stressed that the primary aim of the ashram was not teaching but living; that is, it was to be an integrated life of prayer and action. Jesudason (1937:20-33) also drew from the tradition of modern Hindu ashrams, such as Gandhi's *Satyāgraha* ashram and Tagore's *Sāntiniketan* ashram, to argue that ashrams have adapted to include social service in a life which is integrated, not compartmentalized into religious, political, medical and social spheres. He observed (1937:2-3) that even in the Vedic period the ancient *rishis* carried out experiments in religious ideas and medical science, and that ashrams were places of training for kings.

Both Jesudason and Paton communicated a message of inner-worldly asceticism and selfless action (in the spirit of the *Gītā*) by their dress and life-style. They chose to wear the simple *khadi jibba* and *dhoti* (home-spun cotton shirt and loin-cloth) at a time when this act was a political and social statement of the Gandhian nationalist movement. In fact, it led to Paton's arrest during a *Satyāgraha* protest in Madras in 1932 (Savarirayan, David *et al.,* 1981:32,51). Today, the four ashram members wear *khadi* kurta-pyjama dress. The dress continues to symbolize indigenous asceticism, but it no longer represents a political protest.

The most striking feature of the ashram is the *Jebalayam,* or prayer hall, a stone structure, built in the style of a South Indian Dravidian temple, with two massive *gopurams,* or towers, one over the entrance and one over the sanctuary, each surmounted by a cross. The temple-style prayer hall was constructed and designed, according to Jesudason's inspiration, between 1928 and 1933. There the ashram members, volunteers and visitors gather each day for early morning and evening prayer. The form of prayer is silent meditation or reading of the Gospels, together with use of a Tamil prayer book and a song book of Tamil lyrics set to Indian music. Noon is also observed as a time of prayer, though not by gathering in the prayer hall. Thus the ashramites consciously adopt the Hindu traditional times for *sandhyā* (junction between daylight and dusk, or twilight), and follow an indigenous expression of Christianity. In keeping with evangelical Protestantism, however, there are no images or Indian rituals in the prayer hall.

Silence is an integral part of life, in keeping with the Hindu ashram tradition. Special attention is given to ensuring periods of silence in work, as well as the times of silence for prayer. Despite the many activities of the ashram, the whole atmosphere of this beautiful compound, with countless peacocks stalking the property, on the edge of a bustling Tamilnadu village, is one of solitude and silence.

The activities of the ashram include running a seventy-bed hospital; maintaining the eighty-acre property, in which rice, millet and dahl are grown, and a dairy; conducting a programme of non-formal education; and direct evangelization. The ashram also extends its services to dispensaries and eye clinics in other villages. In addition, it has now developed, as a memorial to the founders, a programme of extension work, the Gurukul or Retreat Centre, for periodic training and orienting of young men for leadership in church and society (Savarirayan, 1981:14). In this aspect of its work, the ashram shows the influence of Gandhi's conception and use of ashrams as training centres.

Christukula ashram has maintained its Gandhian spirit of inner-worldly asceticism and selfless action. Working and living among the villagers, the ashramites and volunteers assert the dignity of manual labour. Their involvement in hospitals, clinics, schools, agriculture and training camps is clear indication of the use of worldly institutions for the sake of promoting the Kingdom of God. Victor (1981:5-6), a member of the ashram, sees ashrams as "bring(ing) religion out of the Cloister into the din and toil of the World," and as having "a significant and symbolic role" as communities where people live and learn "how the Church should live and work in the world of today." The rhetoric of the traditional Hindu way of *karma mārga* has been integrated with that of inner-worldly ascetic Protestantism. The meaning and practice of evangelization have been reinterpreted to meet the circumstances of the changed socio-cultural environment of post-independence India.

Christavashram

Christavashram, an inter-denominational ashram in Mangānam, near Kottayam, Kerala, is also inspired by Gandhiji's principles and "experiments with Truth."[2] The ashram is a conscious attempt to integrate the concepts of Christ's "Kingdom on Earth," Gandhi's "*Rām Rājya*" (the ideal rule of the ancient days of Sri Rāma), and Marx's "Classless Society" (C. Thomas, 1984:3-4). The ashram originated in a Fellowship Group which was founded in the sea-port of Alleppey in 1934 by Sādhu K. I. Mathai, M. P. Job, and K. K. Chandy. Sādhu Mathai was a pioneer of indigenous Christianity and of the Christian ashram movement. He adopted the celibate life and ochre-coloured robe of a Sādhu, while working as an evangelist of the foreign Christian Missionary Society. The origins of the ashram presaged a tension which exists today over the issue of whether celibacy is a necessary condition of contemporary ashram life-style. Sādhu Mathai favoured celibacy, whereas K. K. Chandy did not. When the ashram relocated in 1940 in Manganam as *Christavashram*, it was established as a mixed community, with Sādhu Mathai and Job as celibates, and Chandy as a newly-married man. With the death of Job in 1946, the ashram was clearly defined as a fellowship of families, with Sādhu Mathai fulfilling the *de facto* role of guru of the ashram, despite his insistence that Christ is the only Guru of the Christian ashram.

The conical-style chapel, modelled on a Hindu temple, is a striking indigenous feature of the ashram. There the ashram members meet for *sandhyā* each morning and evening. At noon on working days, members and workers gather in the chapel for Bible study, intercessory prayers and occasional talks. The mode of worship and prayer of the ashram community is typically evangelical Protestantism.

Today, the ashram membership is composed of six families, that is, twelve full-time members who live on the ashram property. There are also twelve associate members who live outside the ashram with their families. Although decision-making is by consensus, an *āchārya* is elected for a three-year term as an administrative leader. Another person may exercise the role of spiritual leadership. The ashram's explicit goal is to live an "intensive community" life as a group of families, for the purpose of evangelism and community service (Thomas, 1965:8, 1984:2). M. M. Thomas (1971-72:6) has identified one of the functions of the ashram as "to foster the prophetic ministry of the Church." The ashram life-style of simple dress, food, housing and community of goods, together with its conscious attempt to realize Gandhi's ideals of non-violence and peace in a Christian context, presents a contemporary expression of Gandhian asceticism. It is also a conscious attempt to carry on Gandhi's practice of putting ashrams in the villages among the people.

In pre-independence India, the ashram participated in Gandhi's *Sarvodaya* (equality and welfare for all) movement, took some initiatives in the *Bhoodan* (land gift) and *Bhavana Dhan* (housing for the needy) movements, and housed a revolutionary youth group called the Youth Christian Council of Action. Today, the principal activity of the ashram is to provide a home and training centre for a hundred destitute and delinquent boys. Over the years, more than a thousand boys have been trained in agriculture, cattle farming, poultry farming, cloth weaving, tailoring, compositor skills, printing, bookbinding, typewriting, shorthand, besides receiving general education. Volunteers assist the ashram members in care and training of the boys. The ashram also runs a Gurukul ecumenical institute for a small number of educated young people, who are given an experience of ashram community life, an opportunity for study of Christianity and other major religions, and training in social and peace movements. In addition, the ashram serves as a venue for numerous meetings, conferences, retreats and seminars of different church groups. It operates a printing press for its own publications and for other organizations. In all, there are one hundred and seventy-five full-time residents of the ashram, associated with the various activities of the ashram, either as staff or inmates. The ashram is in fact a large complex organization, with a heavy emphasis on evangelization. It is not attracting younger members to full-time ashram life, neither among the children of the present family members, nor among others.

Bethel Ashram

Bethel ashram,[3] Kuttapuzha village, Tiruvalla, Kerala, is the mother-house of a community of Church of South India sisters, who have three Bethel branch ashrams in Kerala and three newly-established communities in the state of Andhra Pradesh. In all there are twenty-two full members of the Bethel community, of whom fourteen live at the mother-house in Tiruvalla. Bethel ashram is a member of the Inter Ashram Fellowship. The influence of the Hindu ashram ideal on the structure, life-style and activities of the ashram can be attributed to the missionary experience and contacts of the foundresses, Sister Edith Neve, an Indian-born English woman, and Sister Rachel Joseph, a presbyter's daughter from Kottayam, Kerala. In 1922, both were appointed as missionary teachers among women in the villages around Alleppey, at that time an important trading port. There they were in contact with Sādhu Mathai (1885-1971), a pioneer of the Christian ashram movement, of indigenous expressions of Christianity, and of dialogue with Hindus, who later founded *Christavashram* (Thomas,1971-72:5-6). Living as a celibate *sādhu* in the *kavi* robe which symbolized his renunciation, Sādhu Mathai blended the traditions of *sannyāsa* with evangelical Protestantism.

Bethel ashram dates its origin to 1922, when the missionary foundresses began their work among Christians, Hindus and Muslims in the district around Alleppey. In 1926, the ashram was established at the present site near Tiruvalla. The principles of a simple, celibate life-style were laid down, but the community grew along evangelistic missionary lines rather than according to traditional Hindu ashram patterns. The *khadi* saree of white with blue border, which was adopted by the Bethany sisters as their dress, became the uniform of the Church of South India sisterhood, founded in 1952. Although Bethel ashram is an autonomous society, the ashram members belong to the C.S.I sisterhood. The ashram community has become institutionalized as a typically evangelistic Protestant community with two senior elected authority figures who have a limited term of office. On Sundays, the community worships with the local church.

The original ashram building of 1926 has now developed into a complex of ten cottages, well constructed and laid out amid vegetable patches, palm tress and flower gardens. The ashram relies on financial support from local and foreign benefactors. The activities carried on in the cottages include a Bible training centre, two boarding homes for children, a motherless children's home, a teachers' residence, an industrial centre, a home for retired Bethel members, a nursery school and a crèche, and an old-age home for well-to-do people.

The message of Bethel ashramites today is contained in their motto, "As Seeing Him who is Invisible," and in their principles of "Simplicity, Sacrifice, and Sincerity" according to Gospel norms which stress work for the Kingdom of God (Bethel ashram, 1982). In living out these ideals, they form an empirical ascetic community which is actively involved in a great variety of social service institutions. The links with the Hindu ashram tradition of *karma mārga* are part of the collective history and memory of the present-day ashram community; they are no longer a salient feature of life today.

Ashram Fellowships

Other Protestant ashrams or fellowships belonging to the Inter Ashram Fellowship, such as the Christian Medical Fellowship, Oddanchatram,[4] and its offshoot, the Christian Fellowship Community Health and Rural Development Centre, Ambilikkai, Tamil Nadu, present a similar pattern of inner-worldly ascetic Protestantism integrated with the Hindu ashram tradition of *karma mārga*. These mixed communities of married and single people live a life-style in keeping with that of ashrams. They have simple housing and food, and all material goods are held in common.

The Christian Medical Fellowship was started in the 1940s, in the period immediately prior to independence, under the leadership of a medical doctor, Dr. A. K. Tharien, who had a vision of providing medical services according to Gandhian principles of *swaraj* (self-reliance), *swadeshi* (use of local resources), service, and training people for social service, especially health care, instead of relying upon medical institutions run by foreign missionaries; together with Christian principles of evangelism and reconciliation with God. The work began under primitive conditions and at a very basic level in the villages. The Christian Fellowship Hospital, and the ashram community as such, were founded in 1955. Today, there are eleven permanent and two associate community members, who run a two-hundred-and-forty-bed hospital, with a staff of twenty-one doctors, thirty-four nurses, sixteen volunteers, and sixty nursing students spread over a four-year training programme. The fellowship also has a home for fifteen boys and a retreat centre, and it carries on village development and evangelistic work. Although Dr. Tharien is the designated *āchārya* (leader) of the ashram, ideally there is consensual decision-making within a rationally organized administrative structure.

The Oddanchatram Medical Fellowship established the branch community at Ambilikkai, which has now become independent. The Christian Community Health and Rural Development Centre, with aid from the central and state governments, provides medical care specifically for leprosy, cancer and tuberculosis patients. It also conducts nutrition, development sciences and community health development training programmes, which are recognized by Madurai University. The fellowship numbers seven permanent members, one associate member and two potential associate members. All are committed to evangelistic work, whether on a full-time basis or in conjunction with other activities.

The inspiration for these medical fellowships was provided by Gandhi's *satyāgraha* and *swadeshi* movements. Their life and activities are a conscious attempt of Christian Indians to realize Gandhiji's ideas and example by forming Christian ashrams and fellowships which play a significant role in the ministry of healing (Tharien, 1984:128). As in Gandhi's ashrams, in the medical fellowships *karma yoga*, selfless action, is the way that is followed to salvation and to the establishment of the Kingdom of God on earth (much like the Hindu and Gandhian conception of *Rām Rājya*, that is, the ideal rule of Sri Rāma). The medical fellowships have been conceived and actualized as spearheads of a new kind of society, as Gandhi's ashrams were (Chatterjee, 1983:145). In a period of thirty years, the founding members and their followers have dedicated themselves to a life of asceticism and action, which has in fact created settlements which are provided with comprehensive health care, other social services, and the means for training in medical and social development skills.

Sat Tal Ashram

Sat Tal ashram,[5] founded in 1930 by Dr. E. Stanley Jones, an American Methodist missionary, and Kodaikanal Ashram Fellowship,[6] founded in 1934, with *Sat Tal* as its model, are summer ashrams; that is, people do not stay there all through the year, but come there in the summer months to form an ashram community. Both are situated in spectacular mountainous surroundings. *Sat Tal* (Seven Lakes) ashram is in the Nainital district of the Himalayas. The three-hundred-acre estate with its post-office, church, and ashram buildings of central bungalow, smaller bungalows, and numerous cottages, has its own lake and borders on two other lakes. Surrounded by government forests, it is well described by Jones (1932:1) as "secluded and self-contained;" one still has to walk six kilometres by a short-cut path (or travel by jeep over a longer rocky route) to reach the main building of the ashram proper. According to Taylor (1973:12), the pattern of ashram life and activities, initiated in the summer of 1931, has remained essentially the same every summer. Jones (1932:1) explicitly outlined the purpose of the ashram as being "to yoke the Christian spirit and the Indian spirit." The membership of some twenty-five men and women, Indian and foreign, led a disciplined life. They wore Indian dress, ate vegetarian Indian food, sat on the floor Indian-style for meals and group meetings, and used common Indian vessels for eating. The daily schedule was typical of an ashram, with early rising, morning and evening prayer, study of Hinduism and Islam, discussions and manual work. The mode of prayer, however, was characteristically devotional evangelical Protestant prayers and hymn-singing, with some time for silent meditation.

In founding *Sat Tal* ashram as an indigenous community for evangelism, Jones drew heavily on the Hindu tradition. Taylor (1973:41-57), quotes from Jones' writings of the early twenties and notes his elaboration of the influence of the Indian religious heritage on Christianity: the emphasis on God-realization, on meditation, on the reality of the spirit; the tendency to see God in everything, to simplicity of life with few desires for material goods, to the austere religious discipline characteristic of the *sādhu*. Jones was convinced that Christianity in India had to be "rooted in the soil of India and draw sustenance from the Indian genius and thought;" otherwise it would "always be a foreign, un-naturalistic outside thing and consequently unwelcome" (Taylor, 1973:57). Hence, when the ashram was ultimately registered in 1981 under the Uttar Pradesh Societies Registration Act, the aims and objectives of the ashram were set forth as being "to interpret the Lord Jesus Christ and His Kingdom, the centre of the Christian faith, in indigenous forms."

Sensitive to the heightened nationalistic Indian consciousness of the 1920s and 1930s, Jones was also strongly influenced by Gandhiji's spirit of simplicity, asceticism and service (Jones, 1932:287-91). Jones had lived with Gandhi in his *Satyāgraha* ashram, Sabarmati, in the early 1920s; he also spent several months at Rabindranath Tagore's ashram, *Sāntiniketan,* in 1923 (Taylor, 1973:13). According to Taylor (1973:29), "Stanley Jones took Mahatma Gandhi very seriously. He had known him for long, spent time in his Ashram, and kept in touch by correspondence."

In fact, Jones also founded a year-round urban ashram in Lucknow in the 1930s, soon after the foundation of *Sat Tal* (Jones, 1939:228-33). This ashram was involved in many social activities and in "the training of a new type of Christian servant." Thus he espoused Gandhiji's conception of the ashram as a training centre. Jones (1939:236-37) envisioned ashrams as the germs of a new social order, which he called the Kingdom of God order.

For a period of about fifteen years in the 1950s and 1960s, *Sat Tal* was an ecumenical ashram, when a Greek Orthodox priest, Father Lazarus, and a nun, Sister Lila, collaborated with Stanley Jones to establish a Greek Orthodox community which held its worship (with characteristic Orthodox images, incense and rituals) in a building called "The Upper Room." Father Lazarus was a member of the "circle" of Christians who engaged in yearly dialogue on the encounter of Eastern and Western religions (Klostermaier, 1966). His association with the ashram contributed elements of the *bhakti* devotional tradition of Hinduism. It is significant, perhaps, that a portrait of Sādhu Sundar Singh, a renowned Sikh convert who became a Christian *bhaktā* and mystic of the early twentieth century, holds pride of place beside that of the founder in the library of the ashram.[7] Although a mystic, Sādhu Sundar Singh was a very practical evangelist, who became an important exemplar and teacher for the Protestant ashram movement (Winslow, 1926; Jones, 1926:238).

Today all signs of the devotional Hindu way of *bhakti* are gone. The worship and prayer of the ashram are image-less and ritual-free, The Resident Āchārya, Reverend D. P. Titus, sees the ashram as a place of withdrawal to the forest for meditation, to seek God-realization, with "no idols, no temple worship, no brahmin priests."[8] The Christian ashram, in his view, instead of presenting the Christ of miracle-working and marvels (as Western institutionalized Christianity has done), will present a Christ of *yoga, sannyāsa* and God-experience. With Jesus as the Guru, Christian Indians will form communities of disciples who will seek to be a model transformed society--"the Kingdom of God in miniature" (Titus, 1980:20). Thus he has reinterpreted the founder's message to point exclusively to the way of *jñāna yoga*, or knowledge and meditation.

Yet the membership of *Sat Tal* ashram (whom I did not meet in my spring visit) are clearly involved in the institutions of this world for ten months of the year. They retreat to the Himalayan forest hermitage for meditation and community experience of prayer for only one or two months in the summer. Moreover, they belong to a world-wide association of United Christian Ashrams, which Stanley Jones founded. Titus (1980:20) sees the ashram's role as "prophetic and corrective in society" with a significant part to play through its members in various forms of social service throughout the year.

Mar Thoma Ashrams

The Mar Thoma ashrams are also committed to the way of action. In contrast to the Protestant ashrams I have described, they are not autonomous communities. The complicated relations of the Syrian Church with the low Anglican Church Missionary Society in the late nineteenth century led to the formal establishment of the Reformed Mar Thoma Church in 1887 (Boyd, 1969:8). However, the church membership regards its leader as Abraham Malpan (that is, Abraham, the theological teacher), who attempted to initiate reform in the Syrian Church at the synod of 1836. The reforms introduced involve liturgy and theology, to bring the church more in line with evangelical Protestantism. The adherents of the Mar Thoma Reformed Syrian Church would not accept the supremacy of a foreign prelate, the Patriarch of Antioch, but accepted the evangelistical reforms suggested by Western missionaries (Thaliaparampil, 1979:56-7). The Mar Thoma Syrian Church Evangelistic Association, founded in 1888, actively promotes the evangelical thrust of the church and directly controls all Mar Thoma ashrams.

There are five Mar Thoma ashrams, all founded between 1929 and 1954, and since the latter date, no new ashrams have been founded.[9] George (1974:24) notes that all but one of the ashrams were started through the initiative of laymen. The ashrams are explicitly instruments of evangelism; they engage in social, medical, educational and village development programmes, according to the pressing needs of the people.   George (1974:25) has also observed that the Mar Thoma Evangelistic Association seems to be turning the ashrams into paid-worker institutions, rather than retaining their voluntary member status. The Evangelistic Association in some cases now appoints the person in charge of the ashram and transfers members. Thus the structure and authority patterns of the communities resemble those of traditional church organizations rather than those of a typically autonomous ashram.

In their origin and heyday of development, under the inspiration of such leaders as Bishop Abraham Mar Thoma, who exercised a challenging evangelistic leadership between 1915 and 1947, Mar Thoma ashrams were conceived as autonomous groups for missionary work outside Kerala; much as the Neo-Hindu reform movements of Swāmi Vivekānanda, Rabindranath Tagore, Mahatma Gandhi and Sri Aurobindo Ghose were, in a certain sense, missionary in intent.

The liturgy of the Mar Thoma Church is the same as that of the Orthodox Syrian Church, that is, the liturgy of St. James, with some revisions which take into account the church's interpretation of the Bible. The Mar Thomites, however, are free to use other forms of liturgy besides the Syrian liturgy, and they have inter-communion with the Church of North India and the Church of South India. Their theology is Western evangelical Protestant theology.

Christa Panthi ashram, Sihora, Madhya Pradesh, was founded in 1942. During the latter half of the 1930s, three Syrian theological students at Serampore College, West Bengal, under the leadership of the principal of the college, Dr. C. E. Andrews, formed a fellowship with a view to establishing a missionary-oriented ashram in a backward area outside Kerala. The three theologians, P. J. Thomas, K. T. Thomas and John Verghese, prepared for their mission by each learning appropriate skills. John Verghese spent a year at *Christukula* ashram, Tirupattur, where he learned medical aid in an ashram context; P. J. Thomas learned weaving; K. T. Thomas worked as travelling secretary of the Evangelistic Association. On the death of P. J. Thomas, the team was completed by M. P. Mathew. These three founding members of *Christa Panthi* ashram are still living. Their presence in the ashram community keeps alive the original inspiration and at the same time maintains a measure of autonomy for the ashram under the umbrella of the Evangelistic Association.

Christa Panthi ashram includes a sisterhood. The sisters reside in a separate dwelling in the town of Sihora. The main ashram is a thirty-three acre property six kilometres from the town. The sisterhood was founded in 1947 to fulfill the need for women evangelists among village women. Today, the permanent membership of the ashram includes six men and ten women. In addition, there are twenty-five volunteers or persons considering permanent membership of the ashram. The men wear *kavi* dress; the women, white cotton sarees.

The life-style of the ashramites is inspired by the Hindu tradition of *sannyāsa*. The members take vows of simplicity, celibacy and obedience. They live in austerity and poverty, with goods held in common and with no personal income. Obedience is conceived as obedience to the Lord Jesus, the Guru of the ashram. The āchārya is elected for a three-year term by the permanent members. The ashram members form a fellowship, which is the decision-making body; problems and principles of ashram life are discussed in monthly meetings. The belief of the members is that Jesus, the Guru, must be realized individually in each one; thus they will live out the ashram motto, "Thy will be done."

As I have noted above, the main thrust of the Mar Thoma church and ashrams is evangelism in villages. Over the years, *Christa Panthi* ashram has built up a clinic and a hospital, a harijan school, nurseries in the town and in seven villages, weaving classes for women in the town. Nevertheless, one of the founders expressed the conviction that the real purpose of the ashram is that it be a place for reaching God, so that he may work through the individual ashram members as his instruments. For this ashramite at least, there is a tension between active social involvement and a life of prayer and worship. Though prayer and worship are scheduled at specified times in the daily routine, there is a tendency among some ashramites to neglect prayer at the expense of activities. It is the perception of some members that *karma yoga* has lost the quality of selfless service and has become merely activities. Another founding member perceives worship of God as an ongoing attitude, while he pursues his daily life and activities around the ashram or in evangelism among villagers. Work is emphasized as a religious value. Thus, at *Christa Panthi* ashram the traditional Hindu conception of *karma yoga* has been integrated with the Christian religious orientation of inner-worldly ascetic Protestantism.

Christiya Bandhu Kulam ashram, Satna, Madhya Pradesh, was founded in 1952 in what was formerly called the state of Riva, a state which was closed to Christian missionary work until 1946. The region was perceived as an evangelistic challenge by a group of theological graduates from Kerala. The ashram began as a group of four founding men, only one of whom was married, A. T. Chacko; subsequently the other founders married. Chacko and his wife are the only founders who have remained as members of the ashram. Another married couple who joined the ashram in 1958 completes the present permanent membership of two families. In addition, the Mar Thoma missionary of the Satna parish and his wife live at the ashram and co-operate in its work; a salaried bachelor Mar Thoma evangelist and four other volunteer bachelors assist in village evangelism and village development, with financial aid from organizations such as C.A.S.A. (Christ's Association for Social Action).

Besides evangelism, the major activity of *Christiya Bandhu Kulam* ashram is an English-medium school to the eleventh standard high-school level; Reverend Chacko is manager of the school and his wife is principal. For a year only, the ashram operated a small hospital, which had to close because of lack of medical and nursing staff. The ashram community worships on Sundays with the local parish, sometimes using the Church of North India liturgy. Each morning and evening they pray and sing hymns together. Their evening meal is taken in common. The permanent members share a common purse, with allowances being paid for children to attend secondary school, college and professional training courses. In addition, the community receives a monthly allowance from the Mar Thoma Evangelistic Association.

The secretary of the Evangelistic Association perceives *Christiya Bandhu Kulam* ashram as a failure, insofar as it has not attracted additional permanent members. He attributes its failure principally to the attempt to form an ashram community of families, where the wives had not the same commitment to ashram life and values as the founding (men) theologians. In contrast to those wives who became members of the ashram after its foundation, Mrs. Chacko prepared for her ashram life by spending three years at Bethel ashram, Tiruvalla, prior to her marriage; she also stayed at Christukula ashram, Tirupattur, and participated in one of Stanley Jones' summer ashrams at Sat Tal.

The main focus of *Christiya Bandhu Kulam* ashram has remained direct evangelism. The involvement in the school is primarily as a source of income for the ashram. The withdrawal of members seems to have been related to problems over the asceticism of holding goods and incomes in common. The ideals of the remaining members have continued to be realized as an ascetic life, with involvement in village life and social service institutions.

Christa Sishya Ashram

Contrary to other Orthodox Syrian ashrams, *Christa Sishya* ashram is an Orthodox Syrian ashram which follows the way of selfless action *(karma mārga)*. Situated at Thadagam, near Coimbatore, Tamil Nadu, it has a different history from the other Orthodox Syrian ashrams, and, in consequence, a very different structure and orientation. It was founded on 1 January, 1936, by the Anglican Bishop Herbert Pakenham Walsh, who, in company with his wife Clare, decided to retire from a long and active missionary life and to start an ashram in South India (Varghese, 1961:82-111). He thus proposed to enter the *vānaprastha* stage of life.

The striking outcome of this decision was that the ashram was to be an Orthodox Syrian ashram, not an Anglican ashram. In effect, Bishop Walsh provided the finances, experience and leadership for three young Orthodox Syrian students of Bishop's College, Calcutta, where Walsh was principal, to achieve their goal of establishing a mission-field outside Malayalam-speaking Kerala.[10] They were looking for ways of creating a new kind of community for service and evangelism. Bishop Walsh emerged as the person with the qualities and authority to bring it to fruition. In keeping with his vision of ashram life, Bishop Walsh chose a beautiful site of six and a half acres in a dry valley at the foot of the Nilgiri mountains for the construction of simple huts. The development of the ashram was placed in the hands of the Orthodox Syrian Church, with one of its members as *āchārya*. Bishop Walsh consented to being appointed *guru* of the ashram.

From its foundation, the ashram has resembled Protestant ashrams rather than Orthodox Syrian ashrams. First, it was an ashram of married people, not celibates. Secondly, Bishop Walsh continued to lead a very active missionary life throughout India, concentrating particularly on ministry to the sick, until his death in 1959 (Varghese, 1961:104). The members of the ashram engaged in village uplift work and opened two branch centres. In its first twenty-five years or more, the ashram, although an autonomous community of the Orthodox Syrian Church, was Protestant in its principles and life-style.

Today, the ashram has changed.[11] Both men and women are members, but for the past ten years, celibacy is the rule. The ashram has lost some of its original and long-standing members; it now numbers three men (one of whom lives with helpers at the branch ashram) and four women as full members, together with two or three associate members. Father Jacob, the *āchārya*, is concerned that ashram life is no longer attractive to potential new members, especially the young. Because of the aging membership, the ashram activities now consist mainly in providing facilities for retreats, seminars and camps for church-related groups, rather than in active involvement in village evangelization, health care and uplift work. A staff of doctors, nurses and other personnel operates an ashram Medical Centre.

The life-style of *Christa Sishya* ashram is simple and ascetic. The dwellings are a series of long, low huts, made with mud bricks and woven coconut leaves, built between vegetable patches and paddy fields. The worship and prayer are according to the Orthodox Syrian rite, in the traditional early morning, noon and evening hours. The ashram suggests features of a Gandhian ashram; a young associate member of the ashram, who is aspiring to full membership, clearly emphasizes this dimension in his orientation toward action projects and social involvement in village life. *Christa Sishya* ashram demonstrates the tension which exists within some ashrams between the way of action and the way of meditation.

Conclusion

The ashrams I have described in this chapter illustrate a movement among Christian Indians who follow a path of social involvement, which is oriented toward establishing the Kingdom of God on earth. For the most part, their goal is explicitly evangelistic, as well as being concerned with social service and social change. In their commitment to indigenous lifestyles and structures of social relationships, the traditional Hindu way of *karma-mārga* (selfless action) has been amalgamated with Western inner-worldly ascetic Protestantism. However, a model which proved appropriate and attractive in pre-independence India is evidently less attractive in contemporary post-independence India.

Notes

[1]I first met Dr. Raja Savarirayan, Āchārya of Christukula ashram, at Ashram Aikiya Satsang III, Bangalore, where he was a special guest and presented a paper on the ashram, 19 October, 1983. I visited the ashram, 29-31 October, 1983. My information comes from these contacts and from a copy of the Constitution and Memorandum of Association and Bye-Laws (1946; the ashram was registered at Tirupattur, March, 1946); together with other literature listed as references.

[2]I visited *Christavashram* (registered as the Society of St. Thomas) twice: 16 February, 1984, and 21-23 January, 1985. I interviewed the Āchārya, Rev. P. T. Thomas, and one of the founders, Reverend K. K. Chandy. I also spoke with the other ashram members. At the Ashram Aikiya Satsang III in Bangalore, 19 October, 1983, Raju George, a married ashram member, presented a report on the ashram. My information comes from these sources, together with additional ashram literature.

[3]I visited Bethel ashram, Kattapuzha, Tiruvalla, 22 January, 1985, and interviewed the present Mother, Sr. Chechamma George, and the Assistant Mother, Sr. Sara Thomas. I also met ashram representatives at the Inter Ashram Fellowship annual meeting at Ambilikkai, 11 February, 1984.

[4]I visited the Christian Medical Fellowship, Oddanchatram, and the Christian Fellowship Community Health and Rural Development Centre, Ambilikkai, while attending the annual meeting of the Inter Ashram Fellowship, held at the latter, 10-11 February, 1984. I interviewed the Āchāryas, Dr. A. K. Tharien and Dr. Jacob Cherian, respectively. I also met Dr. Tharien earlier, 19 October, 1983, when he gave a slide presentation and talk on the history, purpose and life of the Christian Medical Fellowship at the Catholic Ashram Aikiya Satsang III, held in Bangalore.

[5]I first heard of *Sat Tal* ashram from Professor John Haysom, a colleague at Saint Mary's University, Halifax, who had lived in India as a young man. From him I learned that it had been associated with the Greek Orthodox Church; hence I was motivated to pursue this link which might otherwise have escaped me. A question relating to this item led Reverend Titus to elaborate on his own contrasting theology and religious orientation. When I visited *Sat Tal* ashram, 27 April to1 May, 1984, I was the sole guest. Only the Āchārya, Rev. D. P. Titus, and the Treasurer, A. M. Chandy, and a skeleton staff, were in residence. My information comes mainly from Reverend Titus, a very articulate speaker, evangelist and writer, as well as from literature about the ashram, which he gave me.

[6]When I visited Kodaikanal, 14 February, 1984, only a caretaker was in residence. However, on 10 February, 1984, at Ambilikkai, I was able to meet and talk with the aged and ailing (and since deceased) Dr. Dick Keithahn (called Richard

Benedict, since he had become a Benedictine oblate and retired to a more contemplative life). The notice of the foundation of Kodaikanal Ashram Fellowship is advertised in *The Guardian* (1934:126,203).

[7]Sundar Singh was a convert to Christianity from Sikhism. In 1905, during the period of religious and social reform movements, he adopted the life of a wandering *sādhu*, with saffron robe and extreme simplicity of life (Neill, 1964:482-83). Like Brahmabandhab Upadhyay, he advocated indigenous theology and living outside the organizational church. In contrast to Brahmabandhab Upadhyay, however, Sundar Singh was primarily a religious guru and teacher (Baago, 1969:50-70). His conversion to Christianity came from an intense religious experience of *samādhi*, or realization of the living Christ within, rather than of an exemplary historical Christ. His method of teaching was through vivid parables (Boyd, 1969:96,109). He also drew on devotional writings, such as *The Imitation of Christ* and the writings of St. Francis of Assisi, besides the gospel. Though a Sikh by birth, he was trained by his mother in the *bhakti* devotional tradition of Hinduism (Boyd, 1969:92). For Sundar Singh, religion meant love and commitment, not knowledge; hence he rejected the way of *jñāna* (knowledge) and also of *karma* (works or action) in favour of the way of the heart, which came closest to *bhakti-mārga* (Boyd, 1969-107-8).

[8]Conversation with Reverend Titus, 30 April, 1984.

[9]I visited two Mar Thoma ashrams in Madhya Pradesh: *Christiya Bandhu Kulam* ashram, Satna, on 25 February, 1985, and *Christa Panthi* ashram, Sihora, 25-26 February, 1985. I interviewed Mrs. A. T. Chacko, Mr. and Mrs. T. T. Oommen, and V. C. Varghese (salaried evangelist) at the former ashram; the three founding members, the treasurer and several of the sisters at the latter ashram. I also interviewed Reverend George Alexander, secretary of the Mar Thoma Evangelistic Association, at his office in Tiruvalla, Kerala, 8 March, 1985.

[10]In the Orthodox Syrian Church Directory, *Christa Sishya* ashram is listed as the "First Foreign *(sic)* Mission Centre of the Church." 'Home' is clearly defined as Kerala, and nowhere else in India.

[11]My information comes from a visit to the ashram, 24 January, 1985, during which I interviewed Father M. K. Jacob, Āchārya, and other ashram members; also from ashram newsletters.

CHAPTER 8

CONTEMPORARY CHRISTIAN ASHRAMS:

THE WAYS OF KNOWLEDGE AND DEVOTION

Most of the Christian ashrams founded by members of the Orthodox Syrian and Catholic Churches are contemplative and monastic in their orientation. As the Orthodox Syrian and Roman Catholic Churches lay stress on ritual and devotional practices in their worship, their ashrams draw not only from Hindu and Christian monastic tradition, but also from the Hindu bhakti movement. The Catholic ashrams have all been founded since the independence of India. The Orthodox Syrian ashrams are of earlier origin.

Orthodox Syrian Ashrams

Although the Protestant Christukula ashram is usually identified as being the first Christian ashram, an Orthodox Syrian ashram, Bethany ashram, has that distinction. Bethany ashram was founded in 1918 in Ranni-Perunad in central Travancore (now Kerala) by Father P. T. Geevarghese, who was influenced by his experience and contacts as a lecturer at Serampore University College in West Bengal between the years 1913 and 1919. There he prepared a group of young Orthodox Syrian Christian seminarians for a monastic life which drew from the traditions of early Christian monasticism, from his contacts with the Anglican Oxford Mission in Calcutta, as well as from the revived ashram tradition of the Neo-Hindu reform movements (Gibbons, 1962:19-31). His aim was a revival of the spiritual life of the Orthodox Syrian Church which would express the awakened nationalist consciousness and be in tune with Indian culture. By 1918 he had acquired the property he desired to establish his ashram at Ranni-Perunad in Travancore. The following year, the Bethany ashram community of *kavi*-robed monks began a contemplative life which combined the external dress and customs of Hindu monasticism with the Antiochene liturgical rite of worship, canonical hours of prayer, Oriental Christian fasts and other practices. The ashram continued as an Orthodox Syrian ashram under Alexius Mar Theodosius after Father Geevarghese (by then Archbishop Mar Ivanios) left the ashram in 1930 to become the founder of the Syro-Malankara rite, which was affiliated with the Roman Catholic Church.

Today, the Malankara Orthodox Syrian Church has five ashrams (called, also, monasteries or dayaras), with a total of one hundred and thirty-two monks, and eight convents, with a total of one hundred and twenty-two nuns; not all of these members, however, are permanently professed. In fact, full profession is made only after many years. All the ashrams are autonomous celibate communities. With the exception of *Christa Sishya* ashram, Thadagam, Tamil Nadu, (which I have described in   Chapter 7), they are all East Syrian communities, located in Kerala. Only *Christa Sishya* ashram belongs to the Inter Ashram Fellowship.[1]

Bethany ashram exists today as a monastic community which still aims to integrate some aspects of Indian culture with Orthodox Syrian monasticism. It has fourteen fully professed members, who all belong to the society of the Order of the Imitation of Christ. The life-style is monastic; the dress of the monks is the characteristic ochre-coloured (but not style) robe of a Hindu renunciate; the liturgy is according to the St. James Orthodox Syrian Malankara rite. An Indian scholar, M. M. Thomas, has described it as "a cross between Eastern monasticism and a Hindu ashram."[2] The most significant influence, however, in the development of the ashram since the departure of Bishop Mar Ivanios and his followers has been that of high Anglican Western monasticism of the Cowley Fathers and the Mirfield Community of the Resurrection. Little remains of the external symbols of Hindu ashrams besides the *kavi* robe and a simple vegetarian diet. The structures of the community and the patterns of authority are those of Western monastic orders.

The monks of Bethany ashram, Ranni-Perunad, all give retreats, spiritual talks, Bible classes and missions, either in the ashram or in colleges or parishes. These activities, together with a large plantation of rubber trees on the ashram property, provide the income of the community. Despite these worldly activities, the monks, in their concentration on union with God in meditation (contemplative prayer), predominantly follow the way of *jñāna-mārga* rather than action in their daily life. In the celebration of the daily Qurbana (the Orthodox Syrian Eucharistic ritual) and the canonical liturgical hours, carried out with loving devotion, the monks also follow the path of *bhakti-mārga.* Their life-style is typically that of ascetic Western monasticism.

Bethany convent, a community of twenty professed sisters and about eight aspirants, novices and junior sisters, is a contemplative sisterhood on Bethany ashram property. It is of much more recent origin than the ashram, the founding sisters having been trained in Sri Lanka for three years by Anglican Sisters of St. Margaret before they settled in Ranni-Perunad in 1943. The sisters wear white cotton religious dress and follow a strict ascetical Western monastic rule, with no suggestion of any Hindu monastic symbols or practices. Since 1959 they have operated a school, and some of the sisters nurse in a hospital owned by the ashram.

They also have a small branch house in Kottayam for student sisters. Despite this involvement in worldly institutions, the sisters have little association with affairs or people of the world, and all contact is strictly regulated by the superior of the community. She is clearly the single monastic authority figure. Their worship and liturgical prayer are the same as those of the Bethany monks, who minister to the community and in some measure exercise a higher authority over the community of sisters.

Two other Orthodox Syrian communities, Mount Tabor Dayara and Mount Tabor Convent, Pathanapuram, are predominantly concerned with operating church institutions, many of them situated on the huge monastery and convent compound. They have a college, schools, homes for the aged and destitute. Some members of the communities reside in these institutions; some reside in other parts of Kerala and even as far afield as Delhi. There are forty-one members of the dayara and forty members of the convent, but only about a third of these are permanently professed. The convent was founded in 1925, prior to the foundation of the dayara. The monks and nuns belong to the Society of the Order of the Sacred Transfiguration. They follow a strict ascetic monastic life, along the lines of high Anglical Western monasticism, English monks and nuns having been the dominant influence in their training. At the same time, they faithfully adhere to Orthodox Syrian liturgical worship and recitation of the canonical hours.

The convent seeks to attract many young members to maintain its institutions. To that end, it receives young girls and trains them to the rigorous ascetic life, with great stress on obedience to a religious superior. At the same time, education is emphasized, with a view to equipping the members with professional qualifications. There is no suggestion of a thrust toward evangelism (as is found among the Mar Thoma Reformed Syrian ashrams) or toward social involvement.

These Orthodox Syrian ashrams, dayaras and convents are maintaining the traditional heritage of the oldest strand of Christianity in India, with accretions of the Anglo-Christian colonial era. They have long since lost the symbols, structures and practices of the traditonal Hindu heritage . There is evidence of malaise among some of the membership, but no leader has emerged to reinterpret the message in more appropriate terms for contemporary Orthodox Syrian Christian Indians.

Catholic Ashrams

Saccidānanda Ashram (Shāntivanam)

Saccidānanda ashram,[3] dedicated to the Holy Trinity, usually referred to as *Shāntivanam* (Forest of Peace), is the oldest Catholic ashram. It was founded in 1950 on the banks of the sacred Kavery river, at Kulittalai, Tamil Nadu, by the two French priests, Abbé Jules Monchanin, who had come to India expressly to begin a contemplative ashram, and Dom Henri Le Saux, a Benedictine monk who shared his vision and joined him in 1948 (Monchanin and Le Saux, 1951; Monchanin, 1974; Mattam, 1974; Davy, 1984). They adopted the names Parâma Arubi Ananda (The Bliss of the Supreme Spirit) and Abhishiktānanda (The Bliss of the Anointed one), respectively. In choosing to call the ashram *Saccidānanda*, the Hindu term for Brahman, the Absolute, who is conceived as *Sat* (Being), *Cit* (Consciousness), and *Ānanda* (Bliss), the founders expressed their intention of identifying with the Hindu quest of the Absolute, and of relating this quest with their own experience of God, in Christ, in the mystery of the Holy Trinity. Initially their life-style and the rule by which it was guided, presented little different from a Western Benedictine monastery, lived out in huts on the banks of an Indian river. But gradually they adopted the *kavi* dress and Indian modes of squatting on the floor and using Indian vessels. No permanent disciples came, however, before Monchanin's death in 1957. Abhishiktānanda, meanwhile, seemed more drawn to the life of a hermit. As I have noted in Chapter 4, Abhishiktānanda was much influenced by two Hindu sages, Sri Rāmana Mahārshi and Sri Gñānānanda, whom he visited between 1949 and 1957. He attributed to these masters of Hindu spirituality his initiation into "the secrets of India" and Indian monastic life.[4] He eventually moved definitively from *Saccidānanda* ashram in 1968 to settle in the Himalayas, until his death in 1973. It was in the Himalayas that Abhishiktānanda attracted his one disciple, who, like Abhishiktānanda, chose the life of a hermit *sannyāsin*.[5]

When Abhishiktānanda left *Shāntivanam*, Dom Bede Griffiths, a Welsh Benedictine who had been co-founder of Kurisumala ashram in Kerala, came from there with two other monks to settle at *Shāntivanam*. Bede Griffiths is guru today of *Shāntivanam*. A prolific writer and an international lecturer and spiritual guide, Bede Griffiths is unquestionably the charismatic personality who attracts many long- and short-term visitors, particularly Westerners, to the ashram. At the time of my visit, there were three permanent members of the ashram and about three other associate members. All the permanent members are men; but the ashram is open to men and women, single or married, as visitors, and even as core members. Dom Bede's vision of the ashram membership is that it will always be but a few *sannyāsis* and a number of devotees--according to his understanding of the Hindu model.

Shāntivanam has developed into several individual huts for the monks and for some visitors, a long low guest building, another building for meals, a library and a beautiful South Indian style temple--all set in the midst of six acres of vegetable and flower gardens, cultivated fields, papaya, mango, palmyra and coconut groves. The setting indeed recalls the descriptions of ancient Hindu ashrams. In external customs also, the ashram community follows traditional patterns of Hindu ashrams, wearing *kavi,* going barefoot, sitting on the floor for prayer and meals, and eating with the hands.

The traditional *sandhyā* (twilight) hours are set apart for silent meditation. The community meets three times a day for prayer in common: in the morning after the silent meditation, when the prayer is followed by the Eucharist; at midday; and again in the evening. The communal prayer is less formal than the monastic recitation of canonical hours. Besides readings from the Bible, in the morning there are readings from the Vedas, the Upanishads and the Bhagavad Gītā; at noon from the Qu'ran and the Granth Sahib; in the evening from Tamil mystics and poets (Griffiths, 1982:24). In addition there are Sanskrit and Tamil *bhajans* (devotional songs); and the day begins and ends with the *ārati* (waving of the light) ceremony before the Blessed Sacrament. Other symbols drawn from the Hindu tradition are also used in the communal prayer time; sandal paste in the morning, as symbol of grace and divinity; the purple powder of kumkumm between the eyebrows at noon, as symbol of the third eye of wisdom; ashes in the evening, as symbol of the impurities burned away to reveal the purified self. Similarly, in the celebration of the Eucharist, various symbols and gestures are used which recall Hindu customs and at the same time signify that the Mass is a cosmic sacrifice.

Authority in the ashram rests with the guru, who represents Christ and also the customary religious superior of a Christian monastery. The ashram is not completely autonomous. Since Catholic ashrams have all been founded by priests, or members of monastic orders or religious congregations, they are all in varying degrees under the authority of a bishop, and, in many cases, also the authority of a higher religious superior. *Shāntivanam* has recently become affiliated with the Benedictine monastery of Camaldoli in Italy. Thus the *sādhakas* and *brahmachāris* of the ashram, when they become *sannyāsis*, will make their solemn profession as monks affiliated with this monastery. In fact, two ashram members have now made that solemn profession and were ordained to the priesthood in January 1986. The following month, a Camaldolese Benedictine noviciate, with five members, was begun at *Shāntivanam*. The linkage seems designed to give the ashram greater freedom to continue to realize union of the Hindu ideal of ashram with the Christian ideal of monasticism. Apparently the possibilities for this development are more likely by this affiliation than by some other church-link within India.

The common *sādhanā* at *Shāntivanam* is prayer, study and manual labour to maintain the community; although outside labour is hired for the cow herd and land cultivation. Hindu methods of meditation and prayer, particularly yoga, are a major focus of study. The ashram is also involved to a certain extent in village social service and development work. There is evidence, therefore, of elements of all three *mārgas (jñāna-, karma- and bhakti-mārga)* being followed at *Shāntivanam*; nevertheless, *jñāna-mārga*, the path of meditation, knowledge of God, wisdom and intellectual discrimination, unquestionably predominates, because it is dominant in the life and message of the guru, Dom Bede Griffiths. *Shāntivanam* expresses a withdrawal from the world 'to enter into the depths of one's being' through a disciplined spiritual life, remote from the concerns of mundane life and major world threats, such as a nuclear disaster. Service of others and concern for social and political problems of India and the world are expressed mainly through prayer. In a sense, the ashram's affiliation with a relatively remote Italian monastery, rather than a local church institution, is symbolic of this attitude.

Kurisumala Ashram

Kurisumala ashram[6] is very different from Shäntivanam, although Dom Bede Griffiths was its co-founder with Father Francis Mahieu, a Belgian Cistercian. Both came independently to India in 1955, lived temporarily at *Shāntivanam*, then began negotiating with Zacharias Mar Athanasius, bishop of the Syro-Malankara rite community of Tiruvalla, Kerala, toward the establishment of an ashram (Āchārya, 1974:147).[7] The ashram was formally established in 1958, with the two founding monks receiving the ochre-coloured *kavi* dress from the Syro-Malankara bishop. Housed in palm-leaf huts of bamboo and jungle timber, they adopted the life-style of Indian *sannyāsis* (Griffiths, 1966:41-47; Āchārya, 1974:147-50).

Kurisumala ashram is situated in the western ghats of Kerala, which is the heart of Syrian Christianity. At an elevation of about 1220 metres, it commands a view of Mount Anamudi, which rises to some 2750 metres. The site was deliberately chosen by the founders for its isolation and grandeur, so that these conditions might evoke an experience of the presence of God.

Silence is an integral part of life in the ashram. A short period of silence follows each service of recited prayer. The practice of silence throughout many of the daily activities is presented by the *āchārya* as a well-tried mode of inner discipline, which facilitates concentration and control of the emotions and which leads one to find God in the cave of the heart (the *guhā*); that is, one's own heart and the heart of another. The writings of the Upanishads and the teachings and practices of Gandhi are invoked to support the value of silence for the votary of truth.

Kurisumala ashram sees itself as an Oriental monastery dedicated to ecumenism and to dialogue. To this end, over the period since its foundation, the community has made a deep study of the Syro-Antiochene liturgical tradition, which they see as more congruous than the Western liturgical tradition with the Indian religious heritage. The fruits of their study and experimentation are the Malankara Liturgy of the Hours (Āchārya, 1982; 1983), which is used for common prayer throughout the day, and the daily *Bhāratiya Pūjā*, a celebration of the Eucharist which integrates Hindu and Christian symbolism. Indian symbolism is used in the place of worship (the *Pūjā Mandapa*)--the altar, vestments, signs and gestures of Christian worship. The Syrian Common Prayer Book is unique in Catholicism, for in each service one or two hymns of the Vedas, Upanishads or Bhagavad Gītā are included.

The *āchārya* lives out his role of teacher. In his daily instructions he teaches that the aim is to practise, as in the Upanishadic tradition, a three-storeyed ascent to divine consciousness: reading or listening to the word *(grāvana),* personal reflection or meditation *(manana)* and the experience of union *(darsana).* He also teaches another typically Hindu form of contemplative prayer, the practice of *japa,* that is, the recitation of a sacred *mantra,* whether audibly uttered, inaudibly uttered or mentally revolved (Kane, 1941:686-87).[8]

An important element of ashram life is the *satsang* (which means literally, a fellowship of the saints), where there will be a sharing of prayer experiences, *bhajan* singing in Malayalam or Sanskrit, and spiritual discourses, given not only by the *āchārya,* but sometimes also by other *sannyāsis* or by visitors.

The *sādhanā* of Kurisumala ashram is directed to the harmonization of *bhakti* (devotion) and *sevā* (service).   The ashram consciously draws on the Gandhian ashram tradition.   Twenty years ago the Kurisumala Milk Supplies Co-operative Society was created with local farmers, and a Family-size Farms Project was initiated.   Visitors to the ashram, whether men or women, share in the work, whether it be 'bread work' (Gandhi's term for manual work), library or secretarial work.   The *sādhaka* (spiritual aspirant) is taught that, in the harmonization of prayer and work, what matters is the quality of one's commitment to one's life-task.

Kurisumala ashram counts twenty-one members, not all of whom live at the ashram, in keeping with the Hindu tradition that a *sannyāsi* is free to wander or go elsewhere as the Spirit moves him; and unlike the Christian monastic tradition that a monk takes a vow of stability to remain in his monastery.   Since its foundation, the ashram has sent out seven offshoots, including *Shāntivanam* ashram.   In contrast to Hindu monastic life, which is essentially individualistic, with authority and obedience being based on the guru-disciple relationship, the monastic life of Kurisumala ashram is communitarian, with authority and obedience being based on the belief that the religious superior represents Christ, the God-man of salvation history (Dhavamony, 1978:48-51).

The life-style of renunciation, the religious practices (such as daily meditation), the *āchārya's* teaching, the atmosphere of silence, the practice of self-control, detachment, truth, non-violence and service are all conscious attempts to integrate traditional and modern Hindu religious beliefs and practices with Christian belief in the mode of ascent to Truth and union with God through the power of the Spirit of Jesus within.   The Christian monastic tradition, as exemplified in the way of life at Kurisumala ashram, differs, however, from Hindu monasticism in that active participation in communal liturgical celebration of the Eucharist and of the canonical hours is central; at no stage in one's advance toward the goal of God-realization is full liturgical life abandoned (Dhavamony, 1978:48-51; Griffiths, 1984:151).

Kurisumala ashram follows the three ways of *jñāna-mārga, bhakti-mārga* and *karma-mārga,* all elements being present in the ashram life-style. The individual ashram members involve themselves in worldly institutions, while methodically practising an ascetic life. At the same time, there is a suggestion of a srong mystical orientation among the members of the ashram, particularly in the liturgical celebrations. Nevertheless, the message communicated by the *āchārya,* Father Francis, emphasizes *bhakti mārga* in the development in depth of a rich Syrian Christian liturgy integrated with the Hindu heritage.

Thirumalai Ashram

Thirumalai ashram, Chunkankadi,[9] in the Kanya Kumari district of Tamil Nadu, has illustrated in its history and development the tension that exists between emphasis on contemplation as against emphasis on social involvement, which is the most critical issue among Christian ashrams, particularly Catholic ashrams. In other words, it brings out into the open the question of whether the ways of *bhakti-mārga* and *jñāna-mārga* are incompatible with *karma-mārga,* or whether all three ways can be followed harmoniously. The ashram was founded in 1971 as an offshoot of Kurisumala ashram, by a *sannyāsi* , with a *brahmachāri* and a *sādhaka* to assist him. Its aim, like that of Kurisumala ashram, is to live a monastic life which is integrated with Indian culture; in particular with the religious and cultural heritage of Tamil Nadu, where the new foundation was made. Hence the community is attempting to develop a Tamil liturgy, within the Latin rite of the Catholic Church. At present, however, English and Malayalam are the dominant languages in worship, communal prayers, and charismatic singing.

The ashram community still consists of three members, of whom the original founding *sannyāsi,* Father Mariadas, is *āchārya.* The ashram serves as a place of solitude and a retreat centre for visitors. It is situated on a hillside, back about half a kilometre from the busy main road between Trivandrum and Nagercoil. Its life-style is typically monastic. Some external Indian customs (such as sitting on the floor for prayer and meals and eating a vegetarian diet with the hands) have been introduced. Its communal prayer services, however, are typically of the Western charismatic Christian style, rather than being an adaptation of the Hindu traditions.

The Thirumalai Social Service Ashram is situated closer to the main road than the original ashram. Father T. James, a Belgian priest and member of the Society of Auxiliaries of the Missions, who came to India thirty-three years ago, is *āchārya* of this ashram, with an extensive team to assist him. At first Father James was a member of the original ashram; however, his vision of the aims and activities of that ashram were different from that of the founders. Ultimately, in 1976, the Social Service ashram became independent of the original community, while retaining close relations with it. Father James began working with the local Kottar Society Service Centre.

Father James believes in a life of silence and contemplation which also shares the life of the people, in this case, farm labourers, fishermen and potters. Over the last ten years or so, the Social Service Centre has initiated and implemented a comprehensive approach to rural development, which includes a co-operative society for pot-making and the provision of good housing for the potters; a clinic, with a hundred and ten clinics in villages, eighty district women's organizations to teach health care, and twenty community organizers; the training of health guides in a one-week course, systematically organized so that three women from each of seven or eight villages come at one time; provision of maternal and ante-natal care.

The development of the Social Service Centre explicitly draws on Gandhian principles for its inspiration. It is an open and mixed ashram, with men and women as members, celibate and married members. Four religious sisters form part of the membership and engage in social work. It is mixed also in the sense that the members aim to integrate contemplation and action. The common liturgical worship of the Eucharist, in English according to the Latin rite, includes some use of Indian symbols and ritual. It is performed in a chapel which has been constructed in indigenous-style architecture. The ashram is open also in the sense that it offers facilities for group retreats, seminars and action-oriented reflection. It is an ashram for training people in the *sannyāsa* of service.

Anbu Vazhvu Ashramam

Anbu Vazhvu Ashramam,[10] Palani, Tamil Nadu, represents an ashram which has apparently achieved a balanced integration of the three ways of *jñāna-mārga*, *bhakti-mārga*, and *karma-mārga*. This ashram was founded in late 1972 by Father Philip Payant, a French-Canadian Holy Cross Father. The inspiration behind the ashram lies in an invitation Father Philip received to join Abbé Jules Monchanin and Dom Henri Le Saux at Shāntivanam in 1954, when Father Philip stayed some time with them. Having lived an active life of service in important administrative positions in his congregation, Father Philip felt free in 1972 to retire to an ashram way of life, much in the style of a *vānaprastha*. He is, however, a *vānaprastha* whose ashram, rather than being in the forest, is in a famous temple town, deliberately not too close to the temple, but in an area where there are some Christians. The site facilitates the founder's goal of dialogue between Christians and non-Christians.

Father Philip's philosophy is that an ashram is a place of relentless quest of the Absolute. This goal is its sole purpose; prayer is the priority. In this he echoes the teaching of Abbé Monchanin, whom he regards as his guru. Symbolic of this philosophy are the pictures of Sri Rāmana Mahārshi and Abbé Jules Monchanin which hang in the main room of the ashram. But a third picture, one of Brother André of Montreal, symbolises the secondary thrust of the ashram; namely, outreach to the poor in a life of simplicity and service.

For six years the ashram was located in three different rented houses in a colony of Palani. When the move to the present site was made in 1978, a thatched-roof house, identical with that of its neighbours, was constructed. Over the years, the six-acre plot has been developed to produce paddy, corn, special green for six cows, vegetables, coconut palms, lime trees, papaya, grapes, ground nuts, and grains -- all with a view to ultimate self-reliance of the ashram. A few buildings have been added: a thatched-roof kitchen-dining room, and the *kutirs* (huts) for guests.

Besides Father Philip, the ashram members are three Tamil young men, one a *brahmachāri* who has lived there for eight years, and two *sādhakas* with shorter periods of membership. Visitors come for varying periods, sometimes even years; twelve candidates have passed through the ashram, five of them becoming *sādhakas*. Nevertheless, the ashram has few permanent recruits. Father Philip is clearly regarded as the *guru* of the ashram. With years of experience in spiritual and administrative responsibility in his religious congregation, he exercises his authority lightly; he also works with a counselling psychologist of Oddanchatram Medical Fellowship.

The spirituality of *Anbu Vazhvu Ashramam* has some of the elements of all three ways: *jñāna-mārga, bhakti-mārga* and *karma-mārga*. Insofar as the ashram is inspired by Gandhian principles, there is an insistence on *karma* (action and service); but, just as all that Gandhi did and said was an aspect of his "experiments with Truth," so too, the action and service of *Anbu Vazhvu* are an expression of the relentless search for God. There is simplicity and informality in the use of indigenous symbols, rituals and music for common prayer services. For personal prayer, Vipassana meditation techniques of intense concentration are practised. The rhythm of life at *Anbu Vazhvu* gives an impression of an integration of prayer and action.

The ashram is an autonomous registered society under the patronage of the Society of the Fathers of the Holy Cross. Autonomy is a reality, the Patron having an advisory function only. There is a General Board of eight members, which includes the ashram members and which meets annually. In its emphasis on the priority of "the relentless quest of the Absolute" and on meditation techniques to achieve this goal, together with its carefully planned life and its conscious attempt to implement Gandhian principles, *Anbu Vazhvu Ashramam* demonstrates the harmonious integration of the three ways to salvation.

Anjali Ashram and Jeevan Dhara Ashram

Two other Catholic ashrams, founded by leaders of the ashram movement, must be mentioned: *Anjali* ashram, Mysore,[11] and *Jeevan Dhara* ashram, Jaiharikhal, in the Himalayas.[12] *Anjali* ashram was founded by Father D. S. Amalorpavadass in 1979 at the same time as he took the newly instituted Chair of Christianity at the University of Mysore. *Jeevan Dhara ashram* is a 1984 offshoot of Vandana Mātāji's *sādhanā kutir* (small cottage for spiritual striving) on the banks of the Ganges, near Rishikesh.

Anjali ashram is the most meticulously planned ashram I have visited.[13] It is far from the idealized conception of an ashram as a spontaneous community. The ashram began as a Christian community located near the university, until the present site at the foot of the sacred Chamundi hill was acquired. During a period of three or more years, the goals and objectives of the ashram were clarified; the new ashram property and buildings were designed, partially constructed, and finally occupied in March 1984.

From the outset, the ashram has served as a centre for meditation and dialogue. In a detailed brochure, Amalorpavadass has spelt out the significance of symbolism expressed in the milieu, layout and buildings, as well as the principles in the ashram ideal and life-style. One of the ashram objectives is a theological and spiritual synthesis in an inculturated architecture and form of celebration. The ashram community numbers seven members: the *guru* (Father Amalorpavadass), five religious sisters, and a lay brother. The aim of the ashram, however, is that it become a multi-religious community of men and women who will offer others the experience of a living Indian spirituality and who will provide a milieu of dialogue and of academic research. The primary aim of the ashram is explicitly stated as spiritual: a relentless quest for the Absolute, an intense and sustained spiritual search, the establishment of God's Kingdom and of a just society (identified as *Rāma Rājya*).

Since the new ashram opened, the most evident function it has performed has been to serve as a centre for experience and training in Indian Christian Spirituality through week-long programmes, with up to sixty participants at a time, most of them religious sisters; although lay persons, clerics, and even a few Hindus, have also participated. The most recent record, for 1985 to 1986, indicates that some five hundred and fifty 'seekers' have attended these programmes. Father Amalorpavadass clearly exercises the role of *guru* and of *āchārya*, in the sense that the ashram is physically and socially constructed by his recognized authority and that he is its spiritual guide, teacher and administrative head. As priest, leading Catholic theologian, liturgist and university professor, he is eminently qualified to fulfil these roles.

Whereas *Anjali* ashram gives the impression of being the ideal ashram, a model text-book case, so to speak, *Jeevan Dhara* ashram, founded by another outstanding leader of the Catholic ashram movement, Vandana Mātāji, is much less formal and more spontaneous in its growth and development. The most striking feature of the ashram is its location on a mountain spur which commands a spectacular view of the Himalayan peaks, one visitor counting as many as one hundred and twelve snow-capped peaks on a clear winter's day. The grandeur of the mountains and the pure air create an atmosphere of awe, silence and prayer, all of which are considered conducive to the way of *jñāna-mārga*.

The core community at the time of my visit consisted of four religious sisters (among them, Vandana Mātāji), a priest and a young lay woman. Over the months, long- and short-term visitors, men and women, married and single, Indian and foreign, Hindu and Christian, have enlarged the community. Here too, as in *Anjali* ashram, the founder is both *guru* and *āchārya*; her authority, recognized and legitimated by several disciples and the community, makes possible the ongoing life of the ashram. The rhythm of ashram life was quickly established: thrice-daily *sandhyā* (worship); silent mornings for prayer, study and work; afternoons open for visitors; evening *satsang* of community and visitors. The principal *sādhanā* of the ashram is spiritual striving, but the *sādhanā* of every member included *karma-mārga* in the initial months of building construction, vegetable and flower garden cultivation, and other activities associated with setting up a new community.

Both *Anjali* ashram and *Jeevan Dhara* ashram contain elements of all three *mārgas*, knowledge, devotion and action, but *bhakti-mārga* seems dominant in each. Great stress is placed on the use of Hindu symbols, gestures and music in all the communal prayer services and *satsangs*. In both ashrams, the *guru* plays an important role as teacher, not only for the ashram community, but also for a wider public, not exclusively Christian, by publishing books and articles. Hence, *jñāna-mārga* is also an important aspect of each ashram's life. Although *karma-mārga* is followed in the daily service of the community, neither ashram is involved in the kind of social service activities which are characteristic of Protestant ashrams. *Anjali* ashram has taken practical steps toward social action on behalf of a settlement of poor families; it has laid a water pipe from its property and fixed a tap on an adjoining *maidan*, which the families claim as land given for house sites by the last Mahārāja of Mysore.

Both *Anjali* ashram and *Jeevan Dhara* ashram, as Catholic ashrams founded by a priest and a religious sister, respectively, are subject to the higher authority of a bishop, and, in the case of the latter ashram, to a religious superior; nevertheless, within this context, there is virtual autonomy for each ashram. In a sense, they are considered as communities "outside the organization" of the Roman Catholic Church; as such, the locus of authority is within the ashram itself for the purpose of experimentation in indigenous liturgical rituals and life-styles and the development of indigenous Christian theology and spirituality.

Finally, both these ashrams have consciously derived their inspiration and modelled their life-style on their interpretation of the Hindu sacred scriptures, and the Vedic, brahmanic and bhakti traditions of Hinduism. Both ashrams (*Jeevan Dhara* more directly than *Anjali* ashram) have been strongly influenced by the Divine Life Society ashram of Swāmi Sivānanda in Rishikesh. Taylor (1977:27-9) has drawn attention to the ongoing influence of the Divine Life Society ashram, first, through its founder, Swāmi Sivānanda, and later through the present guru, Swāmi Chidānanda, on important contemporary Christian ashrams. This Hindu ashram has fostered Hindu-Christian dialogue for nearly fifty years. In 1980, *Sivānandāshram* collaborated with *Jeevan Dhara Sādhanā Kutir* in a consultation with the Catholic Bishops Conference of India Commission for dialogue on ashram living and the *sannyāsa* ideal (Lederle, 1984:108). In the case of *Jeevan Dhara* ashram, Swāmi Chidānanda is a kind of honorary *guru*. The greatest Christian *guru* to influence Catholic ashrams continues to be Abhishiktānanda, as evidenced by the gathering at *Jeevan Dhara* ashram, in December 1985, to celebrate his life and to reflect on his teaching, writings and experience (Vandana, 1986).

Ecumenical Ashrams

Christa Prema Seva Ashram

Christa Prema Seva ashram, Pune,[14] now an ecumenical ashram, is one of the first Christian ashrams. As I have noted in Chapter 4, it was founded in 1927 by an Anglican missionary, Father Jack Winslow. The ashram ceased to exist in 1962, until it was revived in 1972 as an ecumenical ashram by Anglican and Roman

Catholic Sisters. The ashram property and buildings still belong to the Church of North India.

At the time of my visits, the permanent members of the ashram included four Roman Catholic Sisters, three Anglican Sisters of St. Mary the Virgin, and a Church of North India priest; in addition there were three Christian lay women and two Hindu married couples who, as long-term ashramites, formed part of the core community. Visitors, many of them yoga students, of all castes and creeds, Indian and foreign, brought the ashram community to number twenty-five or thirty at any one period of time. One of the Roman Catholic Sisters exercises the role of āchārya. She is clearly head of the community; but she is generally perceived simply as facilitator for surrender to the Spirit in the group, not as *guru*. The community regards the Risen Christ as the only Guru, present among them in Word and Sacrament and by his Spirit in each member of the community. A large poster in the dining area of the ashram proclaims this ideology. The membership thus forms a Christian fellowship, which is the common mode or organization in the Protestant ashrams. The āchārya (or *guru*) has a much less dominant role than he or she has in the best-known Catholic ashrams.

The ashram takes very seriously its ecumenism in terms of worship and inter-religious dialogue. It is authorized by its representative Christian churches (namely, the Church of North India and the Roman Catholic Church) to be a centre of liturgical experimentation for developing ways of worship and scriptural readings more suitable for the Indian cultural context. Hindu scriptures and readings from the Bible are integrated in the liturgical celebrations. Twelve years of experience as an ecumenical community have confirmed that, paradoxical as it may seem, the Eucharistic celebration is the bond of union and the centre of life for the community. The Eucharist is celebrated some days according to the Roman Catholic rite, other days according to the Church of North India rite.

The community has integrated traditional Hindu symbols and rituals in its communal prayer. Three times they meet for the customary *sandhyā*, using the ārati, or waving of light ceremony, in which the sacred Presence in the Eucharist and in each person is honoured. For the Christian, the light is also a symbol of Christ, the light of the world. The ārati ritual is a sign of commitment to witnessing to the light of Christ. The ritual thus symbolises the integration of the contemplative and apostolic aspects of Christian ashram living.

While stressing the centrality of the Eucharistic community prayer, the ashram, nevertheless, also attaches great importance to the experience of God in silent meditation. The twilight hours of *sandhyā* are thus times of silence in the ashram. Many of the ashram members are experienced in yoga and other forms of meditation.

The ashram follows the path of *jñāna-mārga* in a number of ways. Rāmana Mahārshi's image and spirit are honoured in the ashram. His teachings were communicated in *satsangs* with Swāmi Abhishiktānanda in the early days of the ashram's revival. The *āchārya* is a scholar and professor of Hindu philosophy; the priest member of the ashram is a sanskrit scholar. The ashram is characterized by dialogue with Hindus, Buddhists, Muslims and people of various religions, besides different Christian denominations; by research in Indian religions; and by contact with scholars, students and others of many different cultures. In the evening *satsang*, visitors are invited to share their experience of the search for God in their lives, or to reflect with the community on their life experience.

The ashram has also integrated elements of *karma-mārga* in its life-style. It is an urban ashram, set in a busy suburb of Pune. Two ashram core community members teach: the *āchārya* on a part-time basis at a university, another member on a full-time basis in an elementary school. A third member is a full-time tutor sister in a hospital and in its village clinic which teaches preventive medicine and health care. Other members of the ashram give occasional lectures; several members are committed to a literacy programme for women. The ashram has close relations with the Gandhian Stree Shakti movement for spiritual and social liberation of women; and also with a music pandit who has organized a number of *bhajan mandalis* (group hymn-singing) for women.

Christa Prema Seva ashram thus demonstrates a greater social involvement than many of the other important Catholic ashrams. At the same time, this involvement is more at the intellectual and dialogue level than at the level of direct social service, which is characteristic of many Protestant ashrams. Although the ashram is mindful of its founder, Father Jack Winslow, the symbolic guru of the ashram is Swāmi Abhishiktānanda, whose presence and teaching were very influential in the revival of the ashram in 1972. Hence, its present leadership emphasizes *jñāna-mārga* and *bhakti-mārga*.

Jyotiniketan Ashram

Jyotiniketan ashram, Kareli, Bareilly, Uttar Pradesh, is another ecumenical ashram.[15] I have classified *Jyotiniketan* ashram as an ecumenical ashram because its Board of Trustees is ecumenical, it is declared inter-denominational by Deed of Settlement, and it has a history of ecumenism (Rogers, 1957: 1-6). The ashram was founded in 1954 by the Reverend C. Murray Rogers, an Anglican priest member of the Church Missionary Society, who lived there with his family and one other permanent member until 1971. The ashram property was an estate owned by an English family. Rogers acquired the property in 1959 by Deed of Gift. By Deed of Settlement, dated April 9, 1960, Rogers created a Trust "for the management, protection and preservation of the Trust property for carrying out ... the following objects...." These objects include daily worship in the Christian Faith; community living in a simple manner consistent with life among the poor; growth in the knowledge of God and in the spiritual life; service to those living in the surrounding villages; any other form of activity which is not incompatible with the objects stated above. In 1971, the administration of the Trust and of the ashram was handed over to a Franciscan Capuchin priest, Father Deenabandhu, and the Church of North India bishop on the Board of Trustees was replaced by a Roman Catholic bishop.

Father Deenabandhu sees himself in a caretaker role, with his task to carry on the spirit and life-style established by the founder. The living conditions are extremely simple and in keeping with those of the Hindu, Muslim and Christian neighbours of the ashram. The foundation of the ashram was inspired by the ancient Hindu ashramic tradition and by Gandhi's Hindu reform movement (Rogers, 1957:1-6). An intimate friend of Swāmi Abhishiktānanda, who often stayed at *Jyotiniketan*, Murray Rogers also had close affinity with leaders of Catholic ashrams. The ashram served as the venue for two meetings on Hindu-Christian dialogue in the 1960s.[16] Roger's (1957) vision of the ashram community was as "a Family of the Holy Spirit" which included Hindu, Muslim and Christian neighbours. Today, the present community has a similar attitude and exemplifies the same simplicity of life.

The three ashram members are all celibate Catholic men: the *āchārya*, a Franciscan priest, and a founding *sannyāsi* of Kurisumala ashram. Both men and women, of any creed or culture, are received as guests. Over the years of its development, the liturgical celebrations and *sandhyā* worship integrated progressively more of the Hindu scriptures and spirituality. Deenabandhu continues the ashram tradition, stressing particularly the value of authentic *sannyāsa* (renunciation) as a powerful contemporary Christian symbol. With the help of Catholic sisters in the neighbouring *Shānti* ashram, the ashram runs a dispensary. The worship, however, is more typically Franciscan and Western charismatic than Indian, and although *karma-mārga* is followed at *Jyotiniketan* ashram, the way of *bhakti* is dominant.

Conclusion

The Catholic ashrams, which have emerged in India since independence, have all consistently followed the ways of contemplative and devotional spirituality. The leaders have communicated, by their words and their lives, the message that an inculturated Indian Christianity is possible through an integration of Western Christian contemplative spirituality (with its emphasis on following Christ in obedience to the Spirit and those persons who have authority through him) with the Hindu tradition of seeking *moksa* (liberation) by following the way pointed out in the guru-disciple relationship. Catholic ashramites typically embrace the life-style, customs, symbols and dress of complete renunciation *(sannyāsa)*. For many of them, the Hindu way of *jñāna-mārga* is perceived as being most akin to Christian contemplative spirituality. The Second Vatican Council, with its opening up of Catholic ritual and spirituality to inculturation and experimentation, provided the impetus (and legitimation) for the adoption of Hindu devotional symbols and practices which are characteristic of *bhakti-mārga*.

Notes

[1]My information about the Orthodox Syrian Church and ashrams comes from interviews with the Most Reverend Mathews Mar Barnabas, Metropolitan of the Orthodox Syrian Church, Kottayam, Kerala, on January 23, 1985, and with the Most Reverend Dr. Paulos Mar Gregorios, Metropolitan of Delhi and the North, on March 4, 1985; and from visits to Bethany ashram and Bethany convent, Ranni-Perunad, Kerala, March 8 to 10, 1985, and to Mount Tabor dayara and Mount Tabor convent, Pathanapuram, Kerala, March 10 to 12, 1985.

[2]M. M. Thomas made this observation in a personal interview at his home in Tiruvalla, 22 January, 1985. M. M. Thomas provided valuable insights on ashrams in general during this interview.

[3]I first met Dom Bede Griffiths 18-22 October, 1983, when I attended the Catholic Ashram Aikiya Satsang III, Bangalore. I visited *Saccidānanda* ashram, *Shāntivanam*, Kulittalai, from 31 October to November 7, 1983. Dom Bede was readily available for daily interviews about the ashram and about the Christian ashram movement in general. Newsletters of the Ashram Aikiya, up to and including December 1986, regularly contain reports of the ongoing life and activities of the ashram, together with Dom Bede's reflections.

[4]*"Secrets de l'Inde"* was the original title of a manuscript drafted by Abhishiktānanda in 1956 and published after his death as *The Secret of Arunāchala* (Abhishiktānanda, 1979). His meetings with Sri Gñānānanda are described in *Gñānānanda, un maître spirituel du pays tamoul* (Abhishiktānanda, 1970a), which has been translated into English as *Guru and Disciple* (London: SPCK, 1970).

[5]In 1971, Abhishiktānanda met a young Frenchman, Marc Chaduc, who became his disciple and stayed with him on the banks of the Ganges at *Phul Chatti Sevā*, a beautiful secluded ashram on the pilgrim path from Rishikesh to Badrinath. Abhishiktānanda made at least two visits with Marc to *Phul Chatti* and writes of their intense spiritual experience *"en commun."* In June 1973, Abhishiktānanda performed a unique Hindu-Christian monastic initiation *(dikshā)* of Marc into *sannyāsa*, giving him the name Swāmi Ajatānanda. It was at the conclusion of four days in the jungle with his disciple that Abhishiktānanda suffered the heart attack in July 1973, which led to his death the following 7 December (Davy, 1981:195-200). During my two months in Rishikesh, December 1983 to January 1984, I learned many details of the lives of Abhishiktānanda and his disciple, Marc, from a swāmi at Sivānandashram, from Vandana Mātāji, and, above all, from a *Satsang,* held at the Christian Retreat and Study Centre, Rajpur, Dehra Dun, on 7 December, 1983, to commemorate the tenth anniversary of Abhishiktānanda's death. Friends and biographers of Abhishiktānanda (notably, Vandana Mātāji, Father James Stuart and Father John Cole) participated in this *satsang.* I also visited *Phul Chatti Sevā* ashram on 16 December, 1983, and spoke with a swāmi who had known Swāmi Abhishiktānanda and Marc.

[6]The name Kurisumala means 'Hill of the Cross.' I have visited Kurisumula ashram twice: in October 1979 and from 17 to 19 February, 1984. My information has been obtained from these visits, from conversations with Father Francis, and from references which I have listed, in particular, Rodrigues (1983). Father Francis took the name Francis Āchārya when he became an Indian citizen in 1968. I have also discussed Kurisumala ashram with its co-founder, Dom Bede Griffiths.

[7]Kurisumala ashram is, therefore, historically linked with the first Orthodox Syrian ashram, established in 1918 by Mar Ivanios. Mar Ivanios became the initiator of reunion of the Syrian Church with Rome by founding the Syro-Malankara-rite Catholic Church in 1930.

[8]Various Christian writers have studied the concept and practice of *japa* as an appropriate expression of Indian Christian spirituality; among them, Abhishiktānanda (1970b:35), Panikkar (1977:39), Vandana (1984b:*passim*).

[9]I visited Thirumalai ashram, 20-22 February, 1984, and resided at the original ashram. The āchārya, Father Mariadas, was absent during my visit. I interviewed Brother Joseph. I visited the Social Service ashram, the clinic, the pottery, and interviewed Father James and the administrative director of the clinic.

[10]My information about *Anbu Vazhvu Ashramam* was obtained in a visit there, 11-13 February, 1984. I interviewed the āchārya, Father Philip Payant, and the brahmachārin and sādhakas. I also met one of the sādhakas at the Ashram Aikiya Satsang III, Bangalore, where he delivered a report on the ashram, 21 October, 1983. I have read several other reports of the ashram in newsletters, published twice a year by the Ashram Aikiya.

[11]I visited *Anjali* ashram, 14-16 March, 1984, when all the members of the ashram had not yet moved to the new site of the ashram. I interviewed Father Amalorpavadass during that visit. I had met and talked with him about indigenization of Christianity in general, and ashrams in particular, on at least two previous occasions; namely, on my first visit to India in September, 1979, when he was Director of the National Biblical, Catechetical and Liturgical Centre, Bangalore, and had just been named as the first occupant of the Chair of Christianity, University of Mysore, in the previous July; and again at Ashram Aikiya Satsang III, 18-22 October, 1983, when he was elected President of the Ashram Aikiya for the following four years. Other information about the ashram was obtained from ashram members and visitors, and from the ashram's report in the Ashram Aikiya Newsletters, published semi-annually, the latest being December 1986.

[12]I visited *Jeevan Dhara* ashram, Jaiharikhal, 19-24 April, 1984, little more than a week after Vandana Mātāji and the ashram members had moved from *Jeevan Dhara Sādhanā Kutir*, Rishikesh. I stayed in *Jeevan Dhara Sādhanā Kutir* during the month of December 1983, to be introduced to and immersed in the totally Hindu

culture of the pilgrimage and ashram centre of Rishikesh. I have discussed ashrams in general, and the aims and ideals of *Jeevan Dhara* in particular, with Vandana Mātāji on innumerable occasions and in many countries, since I first met her in September, 1979. Newsletters of the Ashram Aikiya, up to and including December 1986, record the ongoing life and activities of the ashram.

13An even more meticulously planned ashram community was *Saccidānanda Prema Sangha* (Society of the Love of God), a figment of the imagination of Father Henry Heras, S.J. In a two-volume manuscript of some nine-hundred pages, Father Heras wrote the Rules and Constitutions of this "religious congregation of Christian *sannyāsis.*" Father Heras founded the Indian Historical Research Institute in Bombay in 1926. His two-volume manuscript dealing with the establishment of the *Sangha* and the proposed ways of following the path of *jñāna-mārga* in order "to present the Catholic Church in Indian garb, not only in all the exterior things but even in the way of thinking, preaching and conversing," is dated 1944. It is held at the Heras Institute, Bombay. The community never had any members. Father Heras makes no mention of Brahmabandhab Upadhyay's writings, but he must have been familiar with them. The manuscript gives the impression of being the product of many years of research and thinking. It is significant only in that it indicates an awareness, prior to Indian independence, of possible ways of developing an indigenous Christian community which integrated Hindu and Christian monasticism.

14I first visited *Christa Prema Seva* ashram in July 1979, during my pilot study of Christian ashrams. I visited the ashram several times during the major research period, to participate in the life, to use its excellent library, to consult the āchārya, Sara Grant, RSCJ, and to obtain introductions to other persons and meetings (15 October, 1983; 13-22 November, 1983; 19 December, 1984). My information comes from these visits, from ashram newsletters, and from other publications (Webb, 1981; Winslow, 1930, 1954).

15I visited *Jyotiniketan* ashram, 25-26 April 1984, and interviewed Father Deenabandhu and one of the other ashram members, as well as the sisters living in nearby *Shānti* ashram. I have a copy of the Deed of Settlement, and several letters written by Murray Rogers to his friends while he lived at *Jyotiniketan* ashram.

16See Chapter 4, footnote 7.

CHAPTER 9

SUMMARY AND CONCLUSIONS

The Christian ashram movement emerged in India in the early part of the twentieth century. It was the product and expression of a new religious and nationalist consciousness which affected Hindus and Christians alike. It emerged among a colonized people who had a new world-view and a readiness for political, social and cultural change. Both Hindu and Christian ashram leaders sought a return to the ancient Hindu ashram tradition in which followers gathered around a holy person, called a *guru*, and thus created an ashram. The early Christian leaders were strongly influenced by the Neo-Hindu reform movements (particularly Swāmi

Vivekānanda and the Ramakrishna movement and Mahatma Gandhi and the Sarvodaya movement) which transformed ashrams into communities committed to social transformation.

Sociologically, an ashram is constructed in the relationship between disciples and a *guru* who exercises charismatic authority. The *guru* communicates a message which addresses the concerns and needs of the disciples, and thus the ashram comes into being and is sustained. The *guru* indicates the way to *moksa* (liberation). Typically, he or she emphasizes one of the three principal ways: *karma-mārga* (action), *bhakti-mārga* (devotion) and *jñāna-mārga* (knowledge). In the Upanishadic tradition, liberation means liberation from the cycle of rebirth and realization of Brahman; in the theistic tradition of the *Bhagavad Gītā*, it means also union with a personal God in love and surrender.

The founders of Christian ashrams were all charismatic personalities whose authority rested on their relationship with followers. The writings, records, log books and the like of the Christian ashram leaders reveal that they formed a loose network of people who interacted with each other, with foreign missionaries, and with Indian and foreign theologians who shared their ideals and experiments with ashram life. For instance, Charles Freer Andews, Jack Winslow and Ernest Forrester Paton participated in a Students Christian Conference in 1920. Jack Winslow and some of his English associates visited Mar Ivanios at *Bethany* ashram on their way from England in 1928; they also visited *Christukula* ashram. Stanley Jones gave a lecture at *Christa Seva Sangh* in 1929 (Winslow, 1930:49). The leaders also visited Gandhiji's ashrams, *Satyāgraha* and *Sevāgrām*; and Gandhi in turn visited some of their ashrams. The evidence indicates that, where there were co-founders of an ashram, the presence of two strong charismatic personalities sometimes created problems. Occasionally a founder withdrew; sometimes another ashram emerged around a former co-founder or disciple.

All the Christian ashrams regard Christ as the true *Guru* of the ashram. The Protestant and Catholic ashrams differ, however, in their attitude to the role of the human *guru*. The Catholic ashrams are more inclined to regard a human *guru* as essential and to accept that authority rests in the *guru*. Sometimes in contemporary Catholic ashrams, however, authority has become institutionalized in a person (an *āchārya*) who has rational rather than charismatic authority. No Catholic ashram is autonomous; all are in some measure under the authority of a bishop. The Protestant ashrams, on the other hand, tend to lay little stress on a human *guru* and to regard the community as the locus of the authority; decision-making is by community consensus. This mode of decision-making has sometimes hindered the creative development of the ashram. Most Protestant ashrams are autonomous.

The evidence of my study of Christian ashrams tends to support Worsley's thesis. The Christian ashrams which emerged in India in the early part of this century were a new religious movement. They represented groups of Christian Indians, and those attuned to the aspirations of Christian Indians, who sought to liberate themselves from foreign Christianity and to create Christian communities in which there was no discrimination on the basis of colour or caste and in which there was a simplicity of life-style which matched that of the poor masses of India. I argue (with Theobald, 1980), however, that charismatic authority can have explanatory value in relation to the emergence of the ashram movement. The Christian ashram leaders drew their inspiration from the Neo-Hindu reformers who founded ashrams for the collective re-shaping of Indian society. They identified with the nationalist movement, with radical youth movements, and with those leaders, above all Gandhi, who demonstrated that the way of renunciation *(sannyāsa)* and the way of selfless action *(karma yoga)* could be wedded in a community to realize liberation *(moksa)* for the individual, fellowship and solidarity for the community *(satsang),* and transformation of society.

I contend, moreover, that focus on authority as a socially constructed relationship can also shed light on the success or decline of the ashram movement, if success be measured in terms of the ability of the movement to attract followers and public support. In the Hindu ashram revival movement, the acceptance and legitimation of the authority of the guru-disciple relationship played a significant role; so too did the leader-follower relationship in the founding of the pre-independence Christian ashrams. In both cases, the message of the leaders struck responsive chords in their audiences (as Worsley, 1968:xviii, has put it). They appealed to the awakened religious and national consciousness of Hindu and Christian Indians, respectively. For example, on the one hand, Vivekānanda, integrating the master's message, led the Ramakrishna movement in the direction of educational and social transformation; Gandhi, in his turn, spearheaded a religio-political nationalist movement. Prior to independence, the ashram leaders attracted followers and found support for their project of life and action. Those who accepted the message of the leaders legitimated the authority relationship and made possible the formation of the ashram community.

In its early history, the Protestant ashram movement was a radical Christian movement. Although the ashram members characteristically embraced the *vānaprastha* stage of life, these ashrams were firmly inserted in the world. Moreover, they turned to the vast rural population of India. The members were committed to an asceticism of service and inspired by an incarnational theology which provided the base for a method of social action (Gandhi's non-violent *satyāgraha*) and which aimed at moral and social transformation. They followed the traditional Hindu path of *karma yoga*.

As the ashrams developed, the message became routinized, the structure and day-to-day organization of the ashram became rationalized and decision-making became institutionalized, either in an elected officer or in community consensus. Both the Protestant ashram movement and the Catholic ashram movement developed characterisitically *within* the established churches, rather than in opposition to them. However, because of their different historical backgrounds and their different perspectives on appropriate ways of indigenizing Christianity in India, Protestant ashrams developed as an inner-worldly ascetic movement committed to social transformation, whereas Catholic ashrams developed as communities dedicated to contemplative and devotional spirituality.

The Mar Thoma ashrams were explicitly created for evangelistic purposes. The founders were Christian Indians who shared the newly awakened positive approach to Hinduism, but who also saw the adoption of Hindu external symbols as a potentially effective mode of evangelism. They retained their reformed Syrian liturgy and their evangelistic Protestant theology, with no adoption of Hindu rituals, prayer forms or sacred writings. For the Mar Thoma Church, in its straitened circumstances of the 1930s and 1940s, ashrams, in which the members lived a simple life with goods shared in common, offered an effective instrument of evangelism and, at the same time, a challenging venture for young dedicated missionaries. Today, the Evangelistic Association, as the major organizer of evangelism, finds that its ashrams are on the decline and fail to attract new members. To meet its primary goal of evangelism, therefore, it commissions salaried evangelists, at times appoints managers of ashrams, and financially supports the ashrams. Where there is a viable community of permanent ashram members, they are free to choose an *āchārya* for an elected term, and the ashramites exercise autonomy in their organization and day-to-day living. Although the Mar Thoma ashramites acknowledge in theory the primacy of God-seeking in ashram life, in practice activities often dominate ashram life, so that *karma yoga* has tended to become solely *karma* (work).

With the achievement of national independence, and the declining influence of Gandhian policies and principles, the Christian ashrams in a sense lost their dynamism. In the Gandhian era, the ashram movement articulated a challenge to simple living and social action. The challenge is no longer there. To a large extent, social services are provided by government agencies. The notion of nationalism as an ideology and a movement has also changed. It no longer means independence from colonial domination, but rather the growth of a technologically developed independent and modern secular state. Increasing secularization and industrialization have brought with them rising aspirations to share in the good life, even among those who are service-oriented. Although many Protestant ashrams have the same ascetical commitment to selfless action, they fail to attract new members. Some ashrams have become social-service oriented rather than social-action oriented ashrams. Radical Christians (both Protestant and Catholic), who seek social transformation, tend to associate themselves with secular peoples' movements. In other words, the message of the Protestant ashram movement tends to fall on deaf ears.

Although the Orthodox Syrian Church established the first Christian ashram, Bethany ashram, the Orthodox Syrian dayaras and convents which exist today show little evidence of the Neo-Hindu reform movements which inspired Father P. T. Geevarghese in Serampore College, Bengal, in the early 1900s. Instead, his other source of spirituality, organizational structure and life-style, namely, Western high church Anglican monasticism, has dominated their development. The dayaras and convents are ascetic communities which are actively oriented to the ongoing maintenance of church institutions (schools, colleges, hospitals and clinics).

At Bethany ashram, Ranni-Perunad, the monks continue to wear a *kavi* monastic-style dress, but Mar Ivanios' specific quality of simplicity in dwelling and life-style has gone. Instead, the monks live in typical institutional-style buildings; there are no individual huts or *kutirs*. The ashram is not open to women, except as daily visitors. The ashrams and convents all follow the Syrian-Orthodox Antiochene rite of worship and formal canonical hours of prayer. However, the spiritual formation of the members is explicitly according to the Western monastic tradition. Some of the Orthodox Syrian leaders have expressed their recognition of the inappropriateness Western monastic structures for the Indian socio-religious context. These leaders look to the emergence of one or more charismatic personalities who will renew the spirit and structure of the Orthodox Syrian communities by drawing on traditional and contemporary Oriental spirituality and prayer forms, such as those of the desert monks. Generally speaking, the Orthodox Syrian ashramites, except for some of the younger members, express little concern for social change and greater social involvement. However, the structures are such (especially for women) that there is little opportunity for change. *Christa Sishya* ashram is the exception among the Orthodox Syrian ashrams. In its life-style and engagement in village development, it resembles Protestant ashrams more than other Orthodox Syrian ashrams and draws on the Gandhian ashram tradition. At present it seems to be under some tension as to the direction it should follow in future development.

The Catholic ashram movement, as I have noted in Chapter 4, emerged in post-independence India among European contemplative monks, priests and scholars who sought to integrate Hindu and Christian spirituality and, in particular, to adapt contemplative Western monastic life to the Indian socio-religious context. The Catholic ashram leaders were students of the Vedāntic path of self-knowledge and they adopted the Indian spiritual tradition of *sannyāsa* (renunciation). They initiated and encouraged religious dialogue among themselves and with Hindus. They attracted a small minority of Catholic Indians, mostly men and women who were priests or members of religious congregations, and who in turn became ashram leaders themselves.

The original Catholic ashrams derived their inspiration from the Vedic tradition, brahmanism and the bhakti movement. The primary goal of the ashram was conceived as the quest of the Absolute. In their emphasis on *sannyāsa* (renunciation), meditation (contemplative prayer) and spiritual knowledge they followed the path of *jñāna-mārga*. However, just as *bhakti* religion, with its emphasis on *pujā*, worship experience, rituals and symbols, became widespread in India, so too the Catholic ashram drew from the Hindu *bhakti* (devotional) tradition in structuring their life and worship. The Second Vatican Council articulated a new Catholic religious consciousness and encouraged experimentation in inculturated Catholic symbols and ritual. Catholic ashrams have been in the forefront in developing an indigenous liturgy which makes use of traditional symbols, such as water, lamps, flowers, incense sticks, salt, the sacred book; rituals, such as *ārati* (the waving of light); Indian music and *bhajans;* postures and gestures, such as sitting cross-legged on the floor, joining the hands in *anjali*; Hindu festivals, such as *divali* (the festival of light).

The goal of liturgical renewal, pioneered in Catholic ashrams, is perceived as the development of spiritual and contemplative life among Indian Christians (Abhishiktānanda, 1968-69: 298). The assumption is that liturgy is the vocal and outward expression of an inner genuine life of prayer. The expectation is that the development of an Indian liturgy will lead to an Indian Christian theology. Thus the Catholic ashrams have tended to emphasise the *bhakta's* devotional surrender to a loving God and the experience of "calm, steady, mystical joy, born of inner moral assurances" (Immanuel, 1950: 169). Catholic religion can integrate the *bhakti* tradition of Hinduism more readily than evangelical Protestantism. Hence, it is not surprising that Catholic ashrams, such as *Shāntivanam, Jeevan Dhara* ashram, *Kurisumala* ashram, *Anjali* ashram, and those of the high church Anglican origin, such as *Christa Seva Sangh* (now the ecumenical *Christa Prema Seva* ashram), have stressed *bhakti-mārga* in their life-style.

The Catholic ashrams have seen a flowering since the All India Seminar on the Church in India Today of 1969. However, there is a tendency to call some Catholic institutions "ashrams" which are in no way different from any convent, rectory, child- care centre, training-centre or other church organization. Aside from these communities, there has still been a significant growth in the number of ashrams which seek to realize an indigenized spirituality and life-style which draws on the Hindu religious tradition. Some of them, however, are prayer-houses established by bishops or religious superiors, rather than spontaneous communities around a *guru*.

The strongest criticism lodged against Christian ashrams, and against Catholic ashrams in particular, is that they are not contributing to the growth of a more just society. Grant (1982: 461) recognizes "the danger of developing ways of worship and spirituality that may be deeply rooted in the brahmanical traditions of the past, but for that very reason . . . alien to the poor and oppressed." Vandana (1982), in the light of her experience as an ashramite for more than ten years, has developed the thesis that there are different ways in which ashrams can participate in the work of justice. She argues that the religious and cultural values of ashram life foster social transformation. Amaladoss (1982: 210-1), while recognizing that there has been a progressive shift from *khadi* to *kavi* in empirical Christian ashrams (the Protestant ashrams now being predominantly oriented to social service and the Catholic ashrams being mostly *kavi*-type), argues, nevertheless, that ashrams can play a major role in the promotion of social justice. He suggests three ways in which this is possible: (1) by building up and being a model of the kind of community every movement for social justice wants to create; (2) by being a place of training in ideals, motivation and method, for those who want to engage in social action (as Gandhi's ashrams were); (3) by playing a leadership role in the promotion of social justice in the community. Amalorpavadass (1984:340-6) also addresses this problem when he looks to the future of Christian ashrams.

Ashrams have become, in effect, a liberal Christian movement within the churches. They are communities which are dedicated to simplicity of life and which offer an alternative life-style. Some of the Protestant ashrams, such as *Christavashram*, explicitly associate themselves with the spirit of intentional communities in other parts of the world. The message of the Catholic ashram leaders tends to appeal to religious men and women, who are already committed by vow to obey an individual, and who are seeking a contemplative simple lifestyle, rather than to lay persons, who prefer more democratic patterns of authority. Catholic ashrams tend to be regarded as communities where experimentation and pioneering, particularly in liturgical renewal, can take place. In a sense, they are regarded as communities "outside the organization" (Traugott, 1978) where experimentation and pioneering in liturgical renewal can take place. They are seen not as replacing but rather as supplementing the regular church organizations.

Some Christian ashrams are attempting to develop Gandhian principles in the contemporary social situation and thus to integrate a life of God-seeking and social action. Gandhi invented a method of action, non-violent *satyāgraha*, which made God's message operational in human life (John, 1984: 465). If contemporary Christian ashrams succeed in this goal of integration, they will achieve the ideal of both Hinduism and Christianity which sees no dichotomy between the sacred and the secular world.

APPENDIX I

HINDU ASHRAMS VISITED

Name of Ashram   *Date of Visit*

Brahma Vidyā Mandir, Paunar, Maharashtra   8-12 November 1983

Sevāgrām Ashram, Wardha, Maharashtra   10 November 1983

Sivānanda Ashram, Rishikesh, Uttar Pradesh26 December 1983-24 January 1984

Phul Chatti Sevā Ashram, Rishikesh, Uttar Pradesh   16 December 1983

Purani Jhadi Ashram, Rishikesh, Uttar Pradesh   10 January 1984

Vashista Guhā, Rishikesh, Uttar Pradesh   15 January 1984

Spiritual Regeneration Movement, Rishikesh, Uttar Pradesh   17 January 1984

Mastaram Baba's Sādhanā Kutir, Rishikesh, Uttar Pradesh   17January 1984

Yoga Niketan, Rishikesh, Uttar Pradesh   18 January 1984

Omkarānanda Ashram, Rishikesh, Uttar Pradesh   19-20 January 1984

Parmath Niketan Ashram, Rishikesh, Uttar Pradesh   19 January 1984

Kanyā Kumāri Sthān, Sakori, Maharashtra   1-2 February 1984

Sri Gñānānanda Memorial Trust, Thapovanam, T.N.   26, 29 February 1984

Rāmanāshramam, Tiruvannamalai, Tamil Nadu   27-28 February 1984

Aurobindo Ashram, Pondicherry, Tamil Nadu   1-3 March 1984

Ānandashram, Kanhangad, Kerala   12-14 March 1984

Ramakrishna Mission, Gol Park, West Bengal   21 March 1984

Sāntiniketan, Bolpur, West Bengal   27-30 March 1984

Bihar School of Yoga, Munghyr, Bihar   3-4 April 1984

Satyāgraha Ashram, Sabarmati, Gujarat   6 March 1985

APPENDIX II

CHRISTIAN ASHRAMS VISITED

Orthodox Syrian Ashrams	Date of Visit
Bethany Ashram, Ranni-Perunad, Kerala	9 March 1985
Bethany Convent, Ranni-Perunad, Kerala	8-10 March 1985
Mount Tabor Dayara, Pathanapuram, Kerala	11 March 1985
Mount Tabor Convent, Pathanapuram, Kerala	8-10 March 1985
Mar Kuriakose Dayara, Pampody, Kerala	23 January 1985
Christa Sishya Ashram, Thadagam, Tamil Nadu	24 January 1985

Protestant Ashrams	
Christukula Ashram, Tirupattur, Tamil Nadu	29-31 October 1983
Christian Medical Fellowship, Oddanchatram, Tamil Nadu	10 February 1984
Christian Health & Rural Development Centre, Ambilikkai	10-11 February 1984
Kodaikanal Ashram Fellowship, Tamil Nadu	14 February 1984
Sat Tal Ashram, Bhowali, Uttar Pradesh	27 April-1 May 1984
Bethel Ashram, Kuttapuzha, Tiruvalla, Kerala	22 January 1985

Mar Thoma Ashrams	
Christiya Bandhu Ashram, Satna, Madhya Pradesh	25 February 1985
Christa Panthi Ashram, Sihora, Madhya Pradesh	25-26 February 1985

Catholic Ashrams

Saccidānanda Ashram, Kulitalai, Tamil Nadu	31 October-7 November 1983
Jeevan Dhara Sādhanā Kutir, Rishikesh	26 November-26 December 1983
Aikiya Alayam, Madras, Tamil Nadu	7-9 & 24-26 February 1984
Anbu Vazhvu Ashram, Palani, Tamil Nadu	11-13 February 1984
Kurisumala Ashram, Vagamon, Kerala	17-19 February 1984
Tirumalai Ashram, Chunkankadi, Tamil Nadu	20-23 February 1984
Tirumalai Social Service Centre Ashram, Chunkankadi	22 February 1984
Om Yeshu Niketan, Vagator Beach, Goa	9-11 March 1984
Anjali Ashram, Mysore, Karnataka	14-16 March 1984
Mariam Mai Ashram, Varanasi, Uttar Pradesh	11-18 April 1984
Yesu Ashram, Varanasi, Uttar Pradesh	13 April 1984
Krist Panthi Ashram, Varanasi, Uttar Pradesh	16 April 1984
Jeevan Dhara Ashram, Jaiharikhal, Uttar Pradesh	19-24 April 1984
Shanti Ashram, Bareilly, Uttar Pradesh	25-26 April 1984

Ecumenical Ashrams

Christa Prema Seva Ashram, Pune, Maharashtra	15 October 1983 13-22 November 1983 19 December 1984
Christavashram, Manganam, Kerala	16-17 February 1984 21-23 January 1985
Jyotiniketan, Kareli, Uttar Pradesh	25-26 April 1984

REFERENCES

Abbott, Walter M. (ed.). 1966. *The Documents of Vatican II*. New York: Guild Press.

Abhishiktānanda (Henri Le Saux). 1958. "Christian *sannyāsis*." *Clergy Monthly Supplement* 4:106-13.

_____. 1959. *Swāmi Parama Arubi Ānandam (Father J. Monchanin) 1895-1957: A Memorial*. Tiruchirapalli: Trichinopoly United Printers.

_____. 1968-69. "Indianising Worship: A Study in Hindu Symbolism." *Word and Worship* 1:298-300, 305-7, 2: 77-9.

_____. 1969a. *Hindu-Christian Meeting Point: Within the Cave of the Heart*. Trs., Sara Grant. Bandra, Bombay: The Institute of Indian Culture.

_____. 1969b. *The Church in India*. Madras: The Christian Literature Society.

_____. 1970a. *Gñānānanda: un maître spirituel du pays tamoul. Récits de Vanya*. Chambéry: Eds. Présence.

_____. 1970b. *Towards the Renewal of the Indian Church*. Ernakulum: KCM Press.

_____. 1974. *Saccidānanda: A Christian Approach to Advaitic Experience*. Delhi: ISPCK.

_____. 1975. *The Further Shore*. Delhi: ISPCK.

_____. 1979a. *The Secret of Arunāchala* . Delhi: SPCK.

_____. 1979b. *Les yeux de lumière. Initiation à la spiritualité des Upanishads*. Paris: Le Centurion.

_____. 1986. *La montée au fond du coeur. Le journal intime du moine chrétien sannyāsi hindou*. Intr., R. Panikkar. Dir., M. M. Davy. Paris: O.E.I.L.

Acharuparambil, Daniel. 1980. "The 'guru' in Hindu tradition." *The Living Word*. 86, 1:3-36.

Āchārya, Francis. 1970. "Reorientation of Monastic Life in an Asian Context." Pp. 109-124 in J. Moffett (ed.), *A New Charter for Monasticism* . London and Notre Dame: University of Notre Dame Press.

Ăchārya, Francis (ed.). 1974. *Kurisumala: A Symposium on Ashram Life.* Vagamon, Kerala: Kurisumala Ashram.

_____. 1982, 1983. *Prayer with the Harp of the Spirit: The Prayer of Asian Churches.* Vols I, II, III. Vagamon, Kerala: Kurisumala Ashram.

Alves, R. 1971. *Religion, Oppression and Freedom.* The William Graham Echols Lectures, Wesley Foundation, University of Alabama.

_____. 1984. *What is Religion?* Trs., Don Vinzant. Maryknoll, New York: Orbis Books.

Amaladoss, M. 1982. "Ashrams and Social Justice." *Word and Worship,* 15: 205-14.

Amalorpavadass, D. S. 1971. *Theology of Indigenization.* Bangalore: National Biblical Catechetical and Liturgical Centre.

_____. 1980. "Emerging new vision of the church in the world and new theological approaches in Asia." *Verbum* 21:279-302.

_____. 1984. "Ashram Aikiya: Whence and Whither? I, II." *Word and Worship* 17:303-8,340-6.

Ananthanarayana, N. 1976. *From Man to God-Man: The Inspiring Story of Swami Sivananda.* New Delhi: Indraprastha Press.

Animānanda, B. 1947. *The Blade: Life and Work of Brahmandhab Upadhyay.* Pref. P. Turmes. Calcutta: Roy and Son.

Anthony, Dick and Thomas Robbins. 1978. "The effect of détente on the rise of new religions: The Unification Church of Reverend Sun Myung Moon." Pp. 80-100 in J. Needleman and G. Baker (eds.), *Understanding the New Religions.* New York: Seabury.

Baago, Kaj. 1969. *Pioneers of Indigenous Christianity.* Bangalore: Christian Institute for the Study of Religion and Society.

Bahin, Shraddhananda. 1970. "Brahma Vidyā Mandir: Monastic Experiment." Pp. 221-34 in J. Moffitt (ed.), *New Charter for Monasticism.* Notre Dame and London: University of Notre Dame Press.

Barker, Eileen. 1986. "Religious movements: cult and anticult since Jonestown." *Annual Review of Sociology* 12:329-46.

Barker, Eileen (ed.). 1982. *New Religious Movements: A Perspective for Understanding Society.* New York and Toronto: The Edwin Mellen Press.

Beaver, R. Pierce. 1965. "Christian ashrams in India." *Christian Century* 82: 887-9.

Beckford, James A. (ed.). 1986. *New Religious Movements and Rapid Social Change*. London, Beverly Hills and Newbury Park, New Delhi: Sage/UNESCO.

Berger, P. 1969. *The Sacred Canopy: Elements of a Sociological Theory of Religion*. Garden City, New York: Doubleday and Co. Inc. Anchor Books.

Bird, F. B. and Frances Westley. 1985. "The economic strategies of new religious movements." *Sociological Analysis* 46:157-70.

Blau, Peter M. 1963. "Critical remarks on Weber's theory of authority." *American Political Science Review* 57:305-16.

Boyd, Robin H. S. 1969. *An Introduction to Indian Christian Theology*. Madras: Christian Literature Society.

Brahmabandhab Upadhyay. 1894-99. *Sophia*. A monthly journal published in Calcutta.

Bromley, David G. 1985. "Financing the millenium: the economic structure of the Unificationist Movement." *Journal for the Scientific Study of Religion* 24:253-74.

Bromley, David G. and Anson D. Shupe. 1980. "Financing the new religions: a resource mobilization approach." *Journal for the Scientific Study of Religion* 19:227-39.

Catholic Bishops Conference of India (CBCI). 1969. *The Church in India Today: All India Seminar*. Bangalore, May 15-25, 1969. New Delhi: CBCI Press.

Chakkarai, V. 1938. "The Church." Pp. 101-28 in D. M. Devasaham and A. N. Sudarisanam (eds.), *Rethinking Christianity in India*. Madras: Sudarisanam Pub.

Chandy, K. K. 1983. *The Christavashram, Manganam: A Quest for Community*. Manganam: Christavashram Press.

Chatterjee, Margaret. 1983. *Gandhi's Religious Thought*. London and Basingstoke: The Macmillan Press Ltd.

Chaturvedi, Benarsidas and Marjorie Sykes. 1949. *Charles Freer Andrews: A Narrative*. Foreword by M. K. Gandhi. London George Allen and Unwin.

Chenchiah, P. 1941. "Āsramas: Critical." Part II. Pp. 113-49 in P. Chenchiah, V. Chakkarai and A. N. Sudarisanam (eds.), *Āsramas: Past and Present*. Kilpauk, Madras: Indian Christian Book Club.

Chenchiah, P., V. Chakkarai, and A. N. Sudarisanam. 1941. *Āsramas: Past and Present*. Christo Samaj No. 2. Madras: Indian Christian Book Club.

Clarke, Sundar. 1980. *Let the Indian Church be Indian*. Madras: The Christian Literature Society.

Cole, W. Owen. 1982. *The Guru in Sikhism*. London: Darton, Longman and Todd.

Cox, Harvey. 1977. *Turning East: The Promise and Peril of the New Orientalism* . New York: Simon And Schuster.

Cronin, Vincent. 1959. *A Pearl to India: The Life of Roberto de Nobili*. London: Rupert Hart-Davis.

Cuttat, Jacques Albert. 1957. *La Rencontre des Religions*. Paris: Aubier.

_____ . 1962. "The spiritual dialogue of East and West." *Clergy Monthly Supplement* 6, 2:57-65.

_____ . 1967. *Expérience chrétienne et spiritualité orientale*. Paris: Descles de Brouwer.

_____ . 1969. "Christian experience and Oriental spirituality." *Concilium* 5, 9 (Nov):60-4.

Das, Sisir Kamar. 1974. *The Shadow of the Cross: Christianity and Hinduism in a Colonial Situation*. New Delhi: Munshiram Mancharlal.

Davy, Marie-Madeleine. 1981. *Henri Le Saux, Swāmi Abhishiktānanda: Le Passeur entre deux rives*. Paris: Les Editions de Cerf.

Devasahayam, D. M. and A. N. Sudarisanam (eds.). 1938. *Rethinking Christianity in India*. Madras: Sudarisanam Pub.

Dhavamony, Mariasusai. 1966. "The religious quest of Hinduism." *Studia Missionalia* 15:65-82.

_____ . 1978. "Monasticism: Hindu and Christian." *Bulletin Secretarius pro non Christianis* 37 131:40-53.

_____ . 1982. *Classical Hinduism*. Documenta Missionalia 15. Roma: Universita Gregoriana Editrice.

Drego, Pearl. 1981. "The mission of the local church and the inculturation of the gospel." *Vidyajyoti* 45:258-65,423-35.

Dumont, Louis. 1960. "World renunciation in Indian religions." *Contributions to Indian Sociology* 4:33-62.

Dumont, Louis and D. F. Pocock. 1957.   "For a sociology of India."
Contributions to Indian Sociology 1:7-22.

Durkheim, Emile. 1964. *The Elementary Forms of the Religious Life.* Trs.,
Joseph Ward Swain. London: George Allen and Unwin Ltd.

Elwin, Verrier. 1964. *The Tribal World of Verrier Elwin: An Autobiography.*
London: Oxford University Press.

Emprayil, Thomas. 1980. *The Emerging Theology of Religions.* Padra, Rewa:
Vincentian Publications.

Farquhar, J. N. 1915. *Modern Religious Movements in India.* New York:
Macmillan.

_____. 1919. *The Crown of Hinduism.* London, Edinburgh, Bombay: Oxford
University Press.

Freud, S. 1964. *The Future of an Illusion.* Trs., W. D. Robson-Scott. Ed.,
James Strachey. Garden City, New York: Doubleday & Co. Inc. Anchor
Books.

Gandhi, M. K. 1922. *Speeches and Writings.* Introduction by Mr. C. F. Andrews
and a biographical sketch. 3rd edn. Madras: G. A. Natesan and Co.

_____. 1929. *The Story of My Experiments with Truth.* Parts 4 & 6. Trs. from
the original in gujarati by Mahadev Haribhai Desai and Pyarelal Nair.
Ahmedabad: Navajiwan Press.

_____. 1951. *Selected Writings.* Selected and introduced by Ronald Duncan.
London: Faber & Faber.

Geden, A. S. 1918. "Renunciation." *Encyclopedia of Religion and Ethics* X:729-
30.

Geertz, C. 1976. "Religion as a cultural system." Pp. 1-46 in M. Banton (ed.),
Anthropological Approaches to Religion. London: Tavistock.

George, Thomas Padinjattethill.   1974.   "A Study of the Ashrams of the Mar
Thoma Church with a view to evaluate its relevance in the task of evangelization
today." B. D. Thesis, United Theological College, Bangalore.

Gibbons, Margaret. 1962. *Mar Ivanios, 1882-1953, Archbishop of Trivandrum:
The Story of a Great Conversion.* Dublin: Clonmore and Reynolds, Ltd.

Gispert-Sauch, George. 1976.   "Exploring the Further Shore." *Vidyajyoti*
40:502-506.

Glock, Charles Y., and Rodney Stark. 1965. "On the origin and evolution of religious groups." Pp. 242-59 in C. Y. Glock and R. Stark, *Religion and Society in Tension.* Chicago: Rand McNally & Co.

Glock, Charles Y., and Robert N. Bellah. 1976. *The New Religious Consciousness.* Berkeley: University of California Press.

Gonda, J. 1965. *Change and Continuity in Indian Religion.* The Hague: Mouton & Co.

Grant, Sara 1972. "The Christa Prema Seva Ashram, Poona."*The Examiner* 123:541-2.

_____. 1982. "The 'Ashram Movement' and Social Justice." *Vidyajyoti* 46: 460-62.

_____. 1984. "Ashrams and ecumenism." *Word and Worship* 17:170-5.

Griffiths, Bede. 1966. *Christian Ashram: Essays towards a Hindu-Christian Dialogue.* London: Darton, Longman and Todd, Ltd.

_____. 1974. "Indian Christian Monasticism." Pp.192-7 in *Prayer.* Bangalore: Theological Publications in India.

_____. 1976. *Return to the Centre.* London: William Collins and Sons.

_____. 1982. *The Marriage of East and West.* London: William Collins and Sons.

_____. 1984. "Christian ashrams." *Word and Worship* 17:150-52.

Gyan, Satish Chandra. 1980. *Sivānanda and His Ashram.* Madras: Christian Literature Society.

Hadden, J. K. and C. E. Swann. 1981. *Prime Time Preachers.* Reading, MA: Addison-Wesley.

Hambye, Edward. 1973. "Robert De Nobili and Hinduism." Pp. 325-34 in G. Gispert-Sauch (ed.), *God's Word Among Men.* Delhi: Vidyajyoti.

Harrison, J. B. 1961. "Europe and Asia: the European Connection with Asia." Ch. XVII in F. L. Carsten (ed.), *The New Cambridge Modern History. Vol. V.* "The Ascendency of France, 1648-88." Cambridge: The University Press.

Heberle, Rudolf. 1968. "Social movements." Pp. 438-44 in D. L. Sills ed., *International Encyclopedia of the Social Sciences. Vol. 14.* New York: The Macmillan Company and the The Free Press.

Immanuel, Rajappan D. 1950. *The Influence of Hinduism on Indian Christians.* Jabalpur: Leonard Theological College.

International Missionary Council. 1938. "The Witness of the Church in relation to the non-Christian religions, the new paganisms and the cultural heritage of the nations." Section 5. World Missionary Conference, Tambaran, Madras, 12-19 December, 1938.

Irudayaraj, Xavier. 1969. "Brahma Vidyā Mandir." *Vidyajyoti* 33:34-6.

Ittyavirah, Sadhu. 1970. "Witnessing as a Catholic Sadhu." Pp. 187-98 in J. Moffett (ed.), *A New Charter for Monasticism.* Notre Dame and London: University of Notre Dame Press.

Jacob, Planthodathil S. 1979. The Experiential Response of N. V. Tilak. *Confessing the Faith in India Series 14.* Madras: Christian Literature Society.

Jenkins, J. Craig. 1983. "Resource mobilization theory and the study of social movements." *Annual Review of Sociology* 9:527-53.

Jesudason, Savarirayan. 1937. *Ashrams, ancient and modern: their aims and ideals.* Vellore: Sri Ramachandra Press.

_____. 1938. "Ashrams." Pp. 215-24 in D. M. Devasahayam and A. N. Sudarisanam (eds.), *Rethinking Christianity in India.* Madras: Sudarisanam Pub.

_____. 1939. "The ashram and its contribution to the christian life." *National Christian Council Review* 59:573-84.

_____. 1940. *Reminiscences of a Pilgrim Life: An Autobiography.* Madras: The Chandler Printing Press.

_____. 1946. *The Constitution of Christukula Ashram, Tirupattur.* Katpadi: Narbeithe Printing Press.

Johanns, P. 1922-34. "To Christ through the Vedānta." *Light of the East* I,3-XII, 7.

John, T. K. 1984. "Satyāgraha and Fast according to Gandhi." *Vidyajyoti* 48:456-66.

Jones, E. Stanley. 1926. *The Christ of the Indian Road.* London: Hodder and Stoughton.

_____. 1928. *Christ at the Round Table.* London Hodder and Stoughton.

_____. 1932. *The Message of Sat Tal Ashram, 1931.* Calcutta: The Association Press.

Jones, E. Stanley. 1939. "The Ashram Movement." Pp. 200-37 in *Along the Indian Road*. London: Hodder and Stoughton.

Kalapesi, Mary. 1964. "Some reflections on the fourth meeting on Hindu and Christian spirituality at Jyotiniketan ashram, April 1964." *Religion and Society* 11, 4:71-76.

Kane, Pandurang Vaman. 1941. *History of Dharma Sastra (Ancient and Medieval Religious and Civil Law)*. Vol. II Part I. Poona: Bhandaskar Oriental Research Institute.

Keithahn, Ralph Richard. 1973. *Pilgrimage in India: an autobiographical fragment*. Madras: Christian Literature Society.

King, Ursula. 1984. "The effect of social change on religious self-understanding: women ascetics in modern Hinduism." Pp. 69-83 in K. Ballhatchett and D. Taylor (eds.), *Changing South Asia: Religion and Society*. Hong Kong: Asian Research Service.

Klostermaier, Klaus. 1966. "Sixth meeting on Hindu and Christian spirituality, Jyotiniketan ashram, January 17-21, 1966." *Religion and Society* 13, 2:72-5.

_____. 1968. "Sanyāsa: A Christian way of life in today's India?" *Indian Ecclesiastical Studies* 7 1:8-40.

Krishnabai. 1964. *Guru's Grace (Autobiography of Mother Krishnabai)*. Trs., Sri Swami Ramdas. Kanhangad: Anandashram.

Lalchhuanliana. 1973. "A Study of Indian Christians: Involvement in the Political Developments in India from 1885 to 1947." M.Th. Thesis. Bangalore: United Theological College.

Lederle, Matthew. 1984. "Ashrams and dialogue." *Word and Worship* 17:108-13.

Liebman, Robert C. and Robert Wuthnow (eds.). 1983. *The New Christian Right: Mobilization and Legitimation*. New York: Aldine Publishing.

Liebman, Robert C. 1983. "The Making of the New Christian Right." Pp. 227-38 in Liebman, Robert C. and Robert Wuthnow (eds.) *The New Christian Right: Mobilization and Legitimation*. New York: Aldine Publishing Company.

Maduro, Otto. 1982. *Religion and Social Conflict.*. Maryknoll, NY: Orbis.

Mandelbaum, D. G. 1970. *Society in India, vol. 2: Change and Continuity*. Berkeley: University of California Press.

Marx, K. and F. Engels. 1964. *On Religion*. New York: Schocken Books.

Mattam, Joseph . 1974. *Catholic Approaches to Hinduism: A Study of the Work of the European Orientalists, P. Johanns, O. Lacombe, J-A Cuttat, J. Monchanin and R. C. Zaehner*. Rome: Pontificia Universitas Gregoriana.

_____. 1975. *Land of the Trinity: Modern Christian Approaches to Hinduism*. Bangalore: Theological Publications in India.

McCarthy, John D. and Mayer N. Zald. 1977. "Resource mobilization and social movements: a partial theory." *American Journal of Sociology* 82:1212-41.

McMullen, Clarence O. 1982. *The concept of guru in Indian religions*. Delhi: ISPCK.

Miller, David. 1980. "Religious institutions and political elites in Bhubaneswar." Pp. 83-95 in Susan Seymour (ed.), *The Transformation of a Sacred Town: Bhubaneswar, India*. Boulder, Colorado: Westview Press.

_____. 1981. "The Divine Life Society Movement." Pp. 81-112 in Robert D. Baird (ed.), *Religion in Modern India*. New Delhi: Manohar.

Monchanin, Jules. 1957. "The Quest of the Absolute." Pp. 46-51 in *All India Study Week, 6-13 Dec., 1956*. Madras: The Madras Cultural Academy.

_____.1974. *Mystique de l'Inde, mystère chrétien: Ecrits et inédits*. Paris: Fayard.

Monchanin, Abbé J., S.A.M., and Dom Henri Le Saux, O.S.B. 1951. *An Indian Benedictine Ashram*. Tiruchirapalli: St. Joseph's Industrial School Press.

Moozoomdar, P. C. 1931. *The Life and Teachings of Keshub Chunder Sen*. 3rd. edn. Calcutta: Nababidhan Trust.

Mü(hlmann), W(ilhelm) E(mil). 1977. "Pacificism and non-violent movements." *Encyclopedia Britannica*. Macropedia 13:845-53.

Mundadan, A. M. 1984a. *History of Christianity in India. Vol. I. From the Beginning up to the Middle of the Sixteenth Century*. Bangalore: Theological Publications in India.

_____. 1984b. *Indian Christians: Search for Identity and Struggle for Autonomy*. Bangalore: Dharmaram Publications.

Needleman, Jacob and George Baker (eds.). 1978. *Understanding the New Religions*. New York: The Seabury Press.

Neill, Stephen. 1964. *Christian Missions*. Baltimore: Penguin.

Osborne, Arthur. 1980. "The nature and function of the guru."*The Mountain Path* 17:129-33.

O'Toole, Michael. 1983. *Christian Ashram Communities.* Pune and Satprakashan Sanchar: Ishvani Kendra.

Panikkar, Raimundo. 1964. *The Unknown Christ of Hinduism.* London: Darton, Longman and Todd.

_____. 1977. *The Vedic Experience: Mantra manjari. An Anthology of the Vedas for Modern Man and Contemporary Celebration.* London: Darton, Longman and Todd.

Parrinder, Geoffrey. 1971. *Dictionary of Non-Christian Religions.* Amershan, Bucks: Hulton Educational Publications.

Pendse, D. R. 1984. *Statistical Outline of India 1984.* Bombay: Tata Services Ltd.

Philip, P. O. 1946. "The place of ashrams in the life of the church in India." *International Review of Missions* 35:263-70.

Philip, T. V. 1982. "Introduction." Pp. 1-22 in T. V. Philip (ed.), *Krishna Mohan Banerjee: Christian Apologist.* Madras: The Christian Literature Society.

Prabuddha Bharata (ed.). 1979. "The guru as spiritual teacher." 84, 7:282-90.

Pyarelal. 1958. *Mahatma Gandhi:The Last Phase.Vol. II.* Ahmedabad: Navajivan Publishing House.

_____. 1971. "Mahatma Gandhi and the ashram movement." *Arunodayam* 27 3(May):24.

Ralston, Helen. 1988 (forthcoming). "Strands of research on religious movements in Canada." *Studies in Religion/Sciences Religieuses* 17, 3(Summer).

Ramana Maharshi. 1972. *Talks with Sri Rāmana Mahārshi.* 3 vols. in 1. Tiruvannāmalai: Sri Rāmanashramam.

Ramirez, Francisco O. 1981. "Comparative social movements." *International Journal of Comparative Sociology.* 22, 1-2:3-21.

Rao, D. P. S. 1972. *Five Contemporary Gurus in the Shirdi (Sai Baba) Tradition.* Madras: The Christian Literature Society.

Rao, Mark Sunder. 1983. "The Goal of Life." *Religion and Society* 30:61-71.

Religion and Society (ed.). 1969. "Report on the consultation of Hindu-Christian dialogue, Bombay, 4-8 January 1969." 16, 2:69-88.

Richardson, James T. 1982. "Financing the new religious movements." *Journal for the Scientific Study of Religion* 21:255-68.

Robbins, Thomas, Dick Anthony, James Richardson. 1978. "Theory and research on today's 'New Religions.'" *Sociological Analysis* 39:95-122.

Robertson, Roland. 1979. "Religious movements and modern societies: towards a progressive problemshift." *Sociological Analysis* 40:297-314.

Rodrigues, Elias B. 1983. "The majestic solitude of Kurisumala." *The Examiner* 134:103.

Rogers, C. Murray. 1957. "A Family of the Holy Spirit." *East and West Review*. Reprint. January: 1-6.

_____. 1965. "Hindu and Christian: a moment breaks." *Religion and Society* 12, 1:35-44.

Sahukar, Mani. 1968. *The Immortal Gurus of Kanya Kumari Sthan*. Sakori: Shri Upasani-Kanya Kumari Sthan.

Satyānanda Saraswati, Swāmi. 1981, 1982. *Teachings of Swāmi Satyānanda Saraswati. Vols. I and II*. Monghyr, Bihar: Bihar School of Yoga.

Savarirayan, Raja. 1981. "Christukula ashram: a historical perspective and prospect." Pp.7-12 in R. Savarirayan et al. (eds.), *Sixty Years in His Keeping, 1921-1981*. Tirupattur, N.A.: Christukula Ashram.

_____, Jaya David, R. S. Gupta and George Raja. 1981. *Sixty Years in His Keeping, 1921-1981*. Tirupattur, N. A.: Christukula Ashram.

Schermerhorn, R. A. 1978. *Ethnic Plurality in India*. Tucson: University of Arizona Press.

Sen, K. M. 1961. *Hinduism*. Harmendsworth, Middlesex: Penguin Books.

Sen, P. K. 1938. *Keshub Chunder Sen*. Calcutta: N. Mukherjee.

Shah, Kanti . 1979. *Vinoba, Life and Mission: An Introductory Study*. Tr., L. O. Joshi. Varanasi: Sarva Seva Sangh Prakashan.

Sharma, Arvind. 1986. "New hindu religious movements in India." Pp. 222-41 in James A. Beckford (ed.), *New Religious Movements and Rapid Social Change*. London, Beverly Hills and Newbury Park, New Delhi: Sage/UNESCO.

Sharpe, Eric J. 1965. *Not to Destroy But to Fulfil: The Contribution of J. N. Farquhar to Protestant Missionary Thought in India before 1914*. Uppsala: Swedish Institute of Missionary Research.

Siauve, Suzanne. 1974. "Présentation." Pp. v-xii in Jules Monchanin, *Mystique de l'Inde, mystère chrétien*. Paris: Fayard.

Singh, Karan. 1983. "Hinduism." Pp. 19-73 in Karan Singh (ed.), *Religions of India*. New Delhi: Clarion Press.

Sivānanda, Swāmi. (n.d.). 'Sādhanā': *Path to Perfection*. Durban: Divine Life Society.

Smart, Ninian. 1968. *The Yogi and the Devotee: the interplay between the Upanishads and Catholic theology*. London: Allen and Unwin.

Stark, Rodney and William Sims Bainbridge. 1979. "Of churches, sects, and cults: preliminary concepts for a theory of religious movements." *Journal for the Scientific Study of Religion* 18:117-33.

Stuart, J. D. M. 1982. "Abhishiktānanda on Inner Awakening." *Vidyajyoti* 46:470-84.

Stutley, Margaret and James. 1977. *A Dictionary of Hinduism: Its Mythology, Folklore and Development, 1500 B.C.- A.D.1500*. Bombay, New Delhi, Calcutta, Madras, Bangalore: Allied Publishers Private Limited.

Subbamma, B. V. 1970. *New Patterns for Discipling Hindus: The Next Step in Andhra Pradesh, India*, South Padadena: William Carey Library.

_____. 1973. *Christ Confronts India*. Madras: The Diocesan Press.

Swaminathan, K. (ed.). 1979. *Rāmana Mahārshi*. New Delhi: National Book Trust.

Taylor, Richard W. 1973. *The Contribution of E. Stanley Jones*. Confessing the Faith in India Series. No. 9. Madras: The Christian Literature Society.

_____. 1977. "From khadi to kavi: toward a typology of Christian ashrams." *Religion and Society* 24, 4:19-37.

_____. 1979. "Christian ashrams as a style of mission in India." *International Review of Mission* 68:281-93.

_____. 1983. "Still Cutting: Ruminations over the CISRS after twenty-five years." Pp. 249-62 in Saral K. Chatterji (ed.), *Essays in Celebration of the CISRS Silver Jubilee*. Madras: Christian Literature Society.

Thaliaparampil, Joseph. 1979. "The Synod of Malanthuruthy (June 1876) and its impact on the Orthodox Syrian Church of India." B. D. Thesis, United Theological College, Bangalore.

Thapar, Romita. 1981. "The householder and the renouncer in the Brahmanical and Buddhist traditions." *Contributions to Indian Sociology* (NS) 15: 273-98.

Tharien, A. K. 1984. "Role of the ashrams in health and healing." Pp.127-8 in *Christavashram and Kerala Balagram: Golden Jubilee Souvenir.* Manganam: Christavashram.

Theobald, Robin. 1980. "The role of charisma in the development of social movements." *Archives de Sciences sociales des Religions* 49, 1:83-100.

Thomas, Abraham Vazhayil. 1974. *Christians in Secular India.* Rutherford, Madison, Teaneck:Fairleigh Dickinson University Press.

Thomas, Cyriac. 1984. "Christavashram completes half a century." Pp.3-4 in *Christavashram and Kerala Balagram Golden Jubilee Souvenir.* Manganam: Nalathra Press and Ashram Press.

Thomas, George. 1979. *Christian Indians and Indian Nationalism, 1885-1950: An Interpretation in Historical and Theological Perspectives.* Frankfurt: Verlag Peter D. Lang.

Thomas, M. M. 1969. *The Acknowledged Christ of the Indian Renaissance.* London: SCM Press.

_____. 1971-72. "Guru Sādhu Mathai." *Arunodayam* 28 12, 1:5-6.

Thomas, P. T. 1965. "Christian Ashrams in India." *Bulletin of the Church History Association of India* 7(March):1-8.

_____. 1971. "Christian Ashrams in India." *Arunodayam* 27 3(March):34-7.

_____. (ed.). 1981. *Vengal Chakkarai vol. I.* Madras: Christian Literature Society.

_____. 1984. "Christavashram and Kerala Balagaram enter their 50th year." Pp. 1-3 in *Christavashram and Kerala Balagram. Golden Jubilee Souvenir.* Manganam: Nalathra Press and Ashram Press.

Titus, D. P. 1980. "Ashrams, Past and Future." Pp. 17-20 in *Sat Tal Ashram: Golden Anniversary, 1930-1980.* Lucknow: Lucknow Publishing House.

Traugott, Mark. 1978. "Reconceiving social movements." *Social Problems* 26:38-49.

Vandana. 1975a. "The guru as present reality." *Vidyajyoti* 39 3:127-30.

_____. 1975b. "The guru as present reality." *Vidyajyoti* 39 8:352-7.

_____. 1978a. "Ashrams." *Word and Worship* 11:15-22.

_____. 1978b. *Gurus, Ashrams and Christians.* London: Darton, Longman and Todd.

Vandana. 1978c. "News and Comments: Ashramites' Satsangh." *Indian Theological Studies* 15:358-66.

_____. 1982. *Social Justice and Ashrams*. Bangalore: Asian Trading Corporation.

_____ 1983. "The ashram movement and the development of contemplative life." *Vidyajyoti* 47:179-92.

_____. 1984a. "Ashrams: some illusions and fears." *Word and Worship* 17:33-40,13.

_____. 1984b. *Nāma Japa: Prayer of the Name in the Christian and Hindu Traditions*. Bombay: Bharatiya Vidya Bhavan.

_____ (ed.). 1986. *Abhishiktananda Sadhana Saptah*. Delhi: I.S.P.C.K.

Varghese, K. 1961. *Herbert Pakenham Walsh: A Memoir*. Delhi: I.S.P.C.K.

Varghese, V. Titus and P. P. Philip. 1983. *Glimpses of the History of the Christian Churches in India*: Madras: The Christian Literature Society.

Victor, Royappa S. 1981. "Christian ashram movement." Pp. 5-6 in R. Savarirayan, J. David *et al.* (eds.), *Sixty Years in His Keeping, 1921-1981*. Tirupattur, N. A.: Christukula Ashram.

Visva-Bhārati . 1951. *Sāntiniketan, 1901-1951*. Calcutta: Visva-Bharati Publishing Dept.

Wallerstein, Immanuel. 1974. *The Modern World-System*. New York: Academic Press.

Wallis, Roy. 1982. "The social construction of charisma." *Social Compass* 29, 1: 25-39.

Wallis, Roy and Steve Bruce. 1984. "The Stark-Bainbridge theory of religion: a critical analysis and counter-proposals." *Sociological Analysis* 45:11-28.

Webb, Andrew. 1981. "The Christa Seva Sangh Ashram, 1922-1934." *South Asia Research* 1:37-52.

Weber, Joseph. 1969. "Jules Monchanin: An Introduction and Two Essays." *Cross Currents* 19:81-88.

Weber, Max. 1958a. *The Religion of India: The Sociology of Hinduism and Buddhism*. Trs. and ed., Hans H. Gerth and C. Wright Mills. New York: Oxford University Press.

_____. 1958b. *From Max Weber: Essays in Sociology*. Trs., ed. and intr., H. H. Gerth and C. Wright Mills. New York: Oxford University Press.

Weber, Max. 1958c. *The Protestant Ethic and the Spirit of Capitalism*. Trs., Talcott Parsons. New York: Charles Seribner's Sons.

_____. 1968. *Economy and Society: An Outline of Interpretive Sociology. 3 Vols*. Eds. Guenther Roth and Claus Wittich. Trs., Ephraim Fischoff *et al*. Berkeley, Los Angeles, London: University of California Press.

Williams, George M. 1981. "The Ramakrishna Movement: A Study in Religious Change." Pp.55-79 in Robert D. Baird (ed.), *Religion in Modern India*. New Delhi: Manohar.

Wilson, Bryan R. 1975. *The Noble Savages:The Primitive Origins of Charisma and Its Contemporary Survival*. Berkeley: University of California Press.

_____. 1979. *Contemporary Transformations of Religion*. Oxford: Clarendon.

Winslow, J. C. 1923. *Narayan Vaman Tilak: The Christian Poet of Maharashtra Builders of Modern India*. Calcutta: Association Press.

_____. 1926. *The Indian Mystic: Some Thoughts on India's Contribution to Christianity*. London: Student Christian Movement.

_____. 1929. *The Rule of Christa Prema Seva Sangha*. Private pub.

_____. 1930. *Christa Seva Sangha*. Westminster, London: Society for the Propagation of the Gospel in Foreign Parts.

_____. 1954. *The Eyelids of the Dawn: Memories, Reflections and Hopes*. London: Hodder and Stoughton.

_____. 1958. *The Christian Approach to the Hindu*. London: Edinburgh House Press.

Wolcott, Roger T. 1982. "Church and social action: steelworkers and bishops in Youngstown." *Journal for the Scientific Study of Religion* 21:71-79.

Worsley, Peter . 1968. *The Trumpet Shall Sound: A Study of 'Cargo' Cults in Melanesia*. 2nd edn. New York: Shocken Books.

Wuthnow, Robert C. 1978. "Religious movements and the transition in world culture." Pp. 63-79 in J. Needleman and G. Baker (eds.), *Understanding the New Religions* New York: Seabury.

_____. 1980. "World order and religious movements." Pp. 57-75 in Albert Bergeson (ed.), *Studies of the Modern World-System* . New York : Academic Press.

AUTHOR INDEX

SUBJECT INDEX

STUDIES IN RELIGION AND SOCIETY